DASH DIET COOKBOOK

The Ultimate Guide to Energy, Weight Loss, and Well-Being to Achieve Optimal Health With 250+ Easy and Delicious Recipes. 2 Meal Plans Included

Robert Kevin Edwards

This bundle consists of the following two books:

LOW-FODMAP DIET COOKBOOK

Find Out How To Improve Your Quality Of Life By Reducing The Impact Of IBS And Other Gastrointestinal Problems With 100+ Delicious And Healthful Dishes To Boost Digestive Health

by Robert K. Edwards

DASH DIET COOKBOOK FOR BEGINNERS

1200 Days Of Low-Sodium Dishes That Can Help You To Reduce Blood Pressure And Boost Health, Without Giving Up Taste. 30-Day Food Plan Included

by Robert K. Edwards

DISCLAIMER NOTICE

PLEASE NOTE THAT THE INFORMATION CONTAINED IN THIS DOCUMENT IS FOR EDUCATIONAL AND ENTERTAINMENT PURPOSES ONLY. EVERY EFFORT HAS BEEN MADE TO PRESENT ACCURATE, UP-TO-DATE, RELIABLE, AND COMPLETE INFORMATION. NO WARRANTIES OF ANY KIND, WHETHER EXPRESSED OR IMPLIED, ARE PROVIDED. READERS ACKNOWLEDGE THAT THE AUTHOR DOES NOT INTEND TO PROVIDE LEGAL, FINANCIAL, MEDICAL, OR PROFESSIONAL ADVICE. THE CONTENT OF THIS BOOK IS SOURCED FROM VARIOUS REFERENCES.

IT IS RECOMMENDED TO CONSULT WITH A LICENSED PROFESSIONAL BEFORE ATTEMPTING TO APPLY THE TECHNIQUES DESCRIBED IN THIS BOOK. BY READING THIS DOCUMENT, THE READER AGREES THAT UNDER NO CIRCUMSTANCES SHALL THE AUTHOR BE LIABLE FOR ANY LOSS, DIRECT OR INDIRECT, INCURRED AS A RESULT OF USING THE INFORMATION CONTAINED HEREIN, INCLUDING BUT NOT LIMITED TO ERRORS, OMISSIONS, OR INACCURACIES.

THANK YOU FOR CHOOSING THIS BOOK!

IF YOU ENJOYED IT, PLEASE CONSIDER LEAVING A REVIEW ON AMAZON, IT WILL TAKE LESS THAN A MINUTE.

PLEASE, SCAN THE FOLLOWING QR CODE WITH YOUR MOBILE.

CONTENT

- ➤ **INTRODUCTION ….. 7**
- ➤ **THE DASH DIET ….. 17**
- ➤ **THE LOW FODMAP DIET ….. 132**
- ➤ **BONUSES ….. 242**

INTRODUCTION

Welcome to **DASH DIET AND LOW-FODMAP COOKBOOK: 2 BOOKS IN 1.** In this comprehensive guide, we embark on a journey toward optimal health and well-being through the powerful combination of the DASH (Dietary Approaches to Stop Hypertension) and Low FODMAP (Fermentable Oligosaccharides, Disaccharides, Monosaccharides, and Polyols) diets. While each diet is explored individually in two separate volumes, this book unveils the synergistic efficacy of integrating both dietary regimens. Within these pages, we will delve into the principles, benefits, and practical strategies for implementing these diets singularly and harnessing their combined potential for transformative health outcomes. With 250 delicious recipes included, along with three unique bonuses sections, prepare to embark on a journey toward vitality, energy, and overall well-being as we unlock the full spectrum of benefits offered by these two remarkable dietary approaches.

THE ANSWER IS A HEALTHY LIFESTYLE

Living a healthy lifestyle is about making conscious choices that prioritize physical, mental, and emotional well-being. At its core, a healthy lifestyle revolves around nurturing the body with nutritious foods, engaging in regular physical activity, managing stress effectively, getting adequate sleep, and avoiding harmful substances.

Nutritious Diet

A healthy diet is the foundation of a healthy lifestyle. It involves consuming a variety of nutrient-rich foods that provide essential vitamins, minerals, and other beneficial compounds necessary for optimal functioning of the body. This includes plenty of fruits, vegetables, whole grains, lean proteins, and healthy fats. By focusing on whole, unprocessed foods and minimizing the intake of refined sugars, saturated fats, and processed foods, individuals can fuel their bodies with the nutrients they need to thrive.

Regular Physical Activity

Physical activity is vital for maintaining overall health and preventing chronic diseases. Regular exercise strengthens the cardiovascular system, builds muscle mass, improves flexibility and balance, and enhances mood and mental well-being. It is recommended to engage in at least 150 minutes of moderate-intensity aerobic activity or 75 minutes of vigorous-intensity aerobic activity per week, along with muscle-strengthening activities on two or more days per week. Incorporating activities such as walking, jogging, swimming, cycling, yoga, or strength training into one's routine can help achieve these goals.

Stress Management

Effective stress management is essential for maintaining a healthy lifestyle. Chronic stress can have detrimental effects on both physical and mental health, contributing to conditions such as hypertension, anxiety, depression, and digestive disorders. Implementing stress-reduction techniques such as mindfulness meditation, deep breathing exercises, progressive muscle relaxation, yoga, tai chi, or spending time in nature can help alleviate stress and promote relaxation and emotional well-being.

Adequate Sleep

Quality sleep is crucial for overall health and well-being. During sleep, the body undergoes essential processes such as tissue repair, hormone regulation, and memory consolidation. Chronic sleep deprivation has been linked to an increased risk of obesity, diabetes, cardiovascular disease, and mental health disorders. Adults should aim for 7-9 hours of sleep per night, prioritizing consistent sleep schedules, creating a relaxing bedtime routine, and optimizing sleep environment for optimal rest and rejuvenation.

Avoidance of Harmful Substances

A healthy lifestyle involves avoiding harmful substances that can negatively impact health. This includes abstaining from tobacco products, excessive alcohol consumption, illicit drugs, and other harmful substances. Smoking tobacco increases the risk of numerous health problems, including heart disease, lung disease, stroke, and cancer. Excessive alcohol consumption can lead to liver disease, cardiovascular problems, addiction, and mental health issues. By choosing to abstain from these substances or moderating their use, individuals can protect their health and well-being.

Embracing a healthy lifestyle is a holistic endeavor that encompasses nourishing the body with nutritious foods, staying physically active, managing stress effectively, prioritizing adequate sleep, and avoiding harmful substances. By making conscious choices to prioritize health and well-being, individuals can enjoy a higher quality of life, improved longevity, and a greater sense of vitality and fulfillment.

THE RISKS OF AN UNHEALTHY LIFE

Leading a healthy lifestyle is paramount for overall well-being and longevity. A healthy lifestyle encompasses various habits and practices that promote physical, mental, and emotional health. This includes maintaining a balanced diet rich in fruits, vegetables, whole grains, and lean proteins, engaging in regular physical activity, managing stress effectively, getting an adequate amount of sleep, avoiding harmful substances such as tobacco and excessive alcohol, and nurturing social connections and relationships.

A healthy lifestyle is not just about the absence of illness; it's about thriving and feeling your best in all aspects of life. When we prioritize our health and well-being, we not only reduce the risk of developing chronic diseases but also enhance our quality of life and overall happiness. Failure to adopt a healthy lifestyle can lead to a myriad of health problems, both physical and mental. Here are some of the health issues that may arise from neglecting to prioritize health and well-being:

Obesity: Poor dietary choices and lack of physical activity can contribute to weight gain and obesity, which are major risk factors for numerous chronic conditions such as heart disease, type 2 diabetes, and certain cancers.

Heart Disease: A sedentary lifestyle, unhealthy diet, smoking, and excessive alcohol consumption can increase the risk of developing heart disease, including conditions like hypertension, coronary artery disease, and heart failure.

Type 2 Diabetes: Unhealthy eating habits, lack of exercise, and excess body weight are key contributors to the development of type 2 diabetes, a chronic condition characterized by high blood sugar levels.

High Blood Pressure: Poor dietary choices, excess salt intake, lack of physical activity, and stress can all contribute to high blood pressure, which increases the risk of heart disease, stroke, and other cardiovascular complications.

Stroke: Hypertension, obesity, high cholesterol levels, and smoking are all modifiable risk factors for stroke, a serious medical emergency that occurs when blood flow to the brain is interrupted.

Cancer: Certain lifestyle factors, such as a poor diet, lack of exercise, tobacco use, and excessive alcohol consumption, can increase the risk of developing various types of cancer, including lung, colorectal, breast, and prostate cancer.

Depression and Anxiety: A sedentary lifestyle, poor diet, lack of social support, and chronic stress can contribute to the development of mental health disorders such as depression and anxiety, which can significantly impact quality of life and overall well-being.

Osteoporosis: Inadequate calcium intake, vitamin D deficiency, and lack of weight-bearing exercise can weaken bones and increase the risk of osteoporosis, a condition characterized by brittle and fragile bones.

Alzheimer's Disease and Dementia: Unhealthy lifestyle choices, such as poor diet, lack of exercise, smoking, and excessive alcohol consumption, can increase the risk of cognitive decline and neurodegenerative diseases like Alzheimer's disease and dementia.

Digestive Disorders: A diet high in processed foods, refined sugars, and saturated fats, combined with a sedentary lifestyle, can contribute to digestive issues such as constipation, bloating, irritable bowel syndrome (IBS), and gastroesophageal reflux disease (GERD).

Adopting a healthy lifestyle is essential for preventing chronic diseases, promoting overall well-being, and enhancing longevity. By making simple yet impactful changes to our diet, exercise routine, stress management techniques, and other lifestyle habits, we can significantly reduce the risk of developing health problems and enjoy a happier, healthier life.

DASH AND LOW FODMAP DIETS

The DASH (Dietary Approaches to Stop Hypertension) diet emphasizes the consumption of fruits, vegetables, whole grains, lean proteins, and low-fat dairy while limiting sodium, saturated fats, and sweets. It aims to reduce blood pressure and promote heart health.

The Low FODMAP diet focuses on reducing the intake of certain carbohydrates that are poorly absorbed in the small intestine and can ferment in the colon, leading to symptoms like bloating, gas, and abdominal discomfort.

It involves avoiding high-FODMAP foods such as certain fruits, vegetables, grains, and dairy products to alleviate symptoms of irritable bowel syndrome (IBS) and other gastrointestinal disorders.

The DASH diet is recommended for individuals looking to improve their cardiovascular health, manage hypertension (high blood pressure), and reduce the risk of chronic diseases such as heart disease and stroke.

The Low FODMAP diet is recommended for individuals suffering from irritable bowel syndrome (IBS) or other gastrointestinal disorders characterized by symptoms such as bloating, gas, abdominal pain, and diarrhea. It can also be beneficial for those with conditions such as small intestinal bacterial overgrowth (SIBO) or fructose malabsorption.

THE SIMILARITIES BETWEEN THE TWO DIETS

The parallels between the DASH and Low FODMAP diets are multifaceted and underscore their shared commitment to fostering optimal health and well-being:

Emphasis on Whole Foods: Both dietary approaches prioritize the consumption of unprocessed, whole foods, including an abundance of fruits, vegetables, and whole grains.

These nutrient-dense foods provide essential vitamins, minerals, and antioxidants crucial for overall health and disease prevention.

Limitation of Saturated Fats: Both diets advocate for minimizing the intake of foods high in saturated fats. These fats, commonly found in red meat, full-fat dairy products, and certain processed foods, are known contributors to cardiovascular disease risk. By opting for lean proteins and healthier fat sources, individuals can support heart health and reduce the likelihood of developing chronic conditions.

Limitation of Added Sugars: Both the DASH and Low FODMAP diets prioritize reducing the consumption of foods with added sugars. Excessive sugar intake has been linked to obesity, type 2 diabetes, and heart disease. By steering clear of sugary beverages, desserts, and processed snacks, individuals can better manage blood sugar levels and promote overall metabolic health.

Promotion of Nutrient-Rich Foods: Both dietary patterns advocate for a diverse and nutrient-rich diet to ensure adequate intake of essential nutrients. Incorporating a variety of colorful fruits, vegetables, lean proteins, and whole grains into meals provides the body with the necessary vitamins, minerals, and dietary fiber to support optimal function and vitality.

Limitation of Sodium Intake: Both the DASH and Low FODMAP diets stress the importance of reducing sodium intake. Excess sodium consumption has been linked to hypertension and cardiovascular disease. By opting for fresh, minimally processed foods and seasoning meals with herbs and spices instead of salt, individuals can better control their sodium intake and support heart health.

Focus on Gut Health: While approached differently, both diets acknowledge the significance of gut health. The DASH diet indirectly supports gut health through its emphasis on fiber-rich foods, which promote digestive regularity and support a healthy gut microbiome. Conversely, the Low FODMAP diet directly targets gastrointestinal symptoms by reducing the intake of fermentable carbohydrates that can trigger digestive discomfort in susceptible individuals.

In summary, while the DASH and Low FODMAP diets may differ in their primary objectives and methodologies, they converge on fundamental principles rooted in whole-food nutrition, moderation of unhealthy components, and prioritization of overall health. By adopting and adapting the shared principles of these dietary approaches, individuals can cultivate a foundation for lifelong wellness and vitality.

WHAT YOU WILL FIND INSIDE

The first book, titled DASH DIET COOKBOOK, provides an in-depth exploration of the DASH diet, followed by a delightful collection of diet-friendly recipes. In the second book, we extensively cover the LOW

FODMAP DIET and present an equally enticing recipe compilation. Additionally, both books include comprehensive meal plans and an array of delectable bonuses awaiting you at the end.

Happy reading!

Robert K. Edwards

DASH DIET COOKBOOK FOR BEGINNERS

1200 DAYS OF LOW-SODIUM DISHES THAT CAN HELP YOU TO REDUCE BLOOD PRESSURE AND BOOST HEALTH, WITHOUT GIVING UP TASTE. 30-DAY FOOD PLAN INCLUDED.

THANK YOU FOR CHOOSING THIS BOOK!
IF YOU ENJOYED IT, PLEASE CONSIDER LEAVING A REVIEW
ON AMAZON, IT WILL TAKE LESS THAN A MINUTE.
PLEASE, SCAN THE FOLLOWING QR CODE WITH YOUR MOBILE

COPYRIGHT ROBERT K. EDWARDS 2024

- ALL RIGHTS RESERVED -

Reproduction, duplication, or transmission of the content of this book is strictly prohibited without the written authorization of the author or the publisher.

In no event shall the publisher or the author be liable for any damages, compensations, or monetary losses arising from the information contained in this book, whether directly or indirectly.

You are responsible for your own choices, actions, and outcomes.

Images by Freepik.com

DISCLAIMER NOTICE

Please note that the information contained in this document is for educational and entertainment purposes only. Every effort has been made to present accurate, up-to-date, reliable, and complete information. No warranties of any kind, whether expressed or implied, are provided. Readers acknowledge that the author does not intend to provide legal, financial, medical, or professional advice. The content of this book is sourced from various references.

It is recommended to consult with a licensed professional before attempting to apply the techniques described in this book.

By reading this document, the reader agrees that under no circumstances shall the author be liable for any loss, direct or indirect, incurred as a result of using the information contained herein, including but not limited to errors, omissions, or inaccuracies.

PART ONE: THE OVERVIEW 24

INTRODUCTION.............25
WHAT IS DASH DIET.............26
THE HEALTH BENEFITS OF THE DASH DIET.............35
THE DASH DIET FOOD.............43
FAQ.............51

PART TWO: THE RECIPES.............54

BREAKFAST.............55

BERRY-ALMOND SMOOTHIE BOWL.............56
SPINACH & EGG SCRAMBLE WITH RASPBERRIES.............57
PINEAPPLE GREEN SMOOTHIE.............58
CHOCOLATE-BANANA PROTEIN SMOOTHIE.............59
RASPBERRY YOGURT CEREAL BOWL.............60
SPINACH & EGG TACOS.............61
REALLY GREEN SMOOTHIE.............62
FRUIT & YOGURT SMOOTHIE.............63
BREAKFAST SALAD WITH EGG & SALSA VERDE VINAIGRETTE.............64
MANGO-GINGER SMOOTHIE.............65
WHITE BEAN & AVOCADO TOAST.............66
VEGAN SMOOTHIE BOWL.............67
PEANUT BUTTER-BANANA CINNAMON TOAST.............68
CANTALOUPE SMOOTHIE.............69
SPINACH-AVOCADO SMOOTHIE.............70

MEAL.............71

CHIPOTLE-LIME CAULIFLOWER TACO BOWLS.............72
VEGGIE & HUMMUS SANDWICH.............73
SPINACH & STRAWBERRY MEAL-PREP SALAD.............74
SMOKED SALMON SALAD NICOISE.............75
SWEET POTATO, KALE & CHICKEN SALAD WITH PEANUT DRESSING.............76
MEAL-PREP VEGAN LETTUCE WRAPS.............77
MASON JAR POWER SALAD WITH CHICKPEAS & TUNA.............78
WINTER KALE & QUINOA SALAD WITH AVOCADO.............79
VEGAN SUPERFOOD GRAIN BOWLS.............80
SLOW-COOKER CHICKEN & CHICKPEA SOUP.............81
ROASTED ROOT VEGETABLES WITH GOAT CHEESE POLENTA.............82
EGGPLANT PARMESAN.............83
CHICKEN-QUINOA BOWL WITH OLIVES & CUCUMBER.............84
WALNUT-ROSEMARY CRUSTED SALMON.............85
HASSELBACK EGGPLANT PARMESAN.............86
CHICKEN & VEGETABLE PENNE WITH PARSLEY-WALNUT PESTO.............87
SHEET-PAN CHICKEN WITH ROASTED SPRING VEGETABLES & LEMON.............88
CHICKEN CAESAR PASTA SALAD.............89
DIJON SALMON WITH GREEN BEAN PILAF.............90
SLOW-COOKER VEGETARIAN BOLOGNESE.............91
CREAMY LEMON PASTA WITH SHRIMP.............92
ROASTED SALMON WITH SMOKY CHICKPEAS & GREENS.............93
SLOW-COOKER VEGETARIAN BOLOGNESE.............94
SALMON COUSCOUS SALAD.............95

QUINOA POWER SALAD..............96
SLOW-COOKER CHICKEN & ORZO WITH TOMATOES & OLIVES..............97
SALMON & ASPARAGUS WITH LEMON-GARLIC BUTTER SAUCE..............98
ONE-POT GARLICKY SHRIMP & SPINACH..............99
FIG & GOAT CHEESE SALAD..............100
CHICKEN PESTO PASTA WITH ASPARAGUS..............101
EASY SALMON CAKES..............102
SWEET POTATO CARBONARA WITH SPINACH & MUSHROOMS..............103
CORIANDER-&-LEMON-CRUSTED SALMON..............104
HALZENUT-PARSLEY ROAST TILAPIA..............105
MIZED VEGETABLE SALAD WITH LIME DRESSING..............106

SNACKS..............107

APRICOT-SUNFLOWER GRANOLA BARS..............108
TRADITIONAL GREEK TAHINI DIP..............109
CHERRY-COCOA-PISTACHIO ENERGY BALLS..............110
AIR-FRYER SWEET POTATO CHIPS..............111
TUNA SALAD SPREAD..............112
KALE CHIPS 113
VEGAN CHOCOLATE-DIPPED..............114
FRUIT ENERGY BALLS..............115
ROASTED BEET HUMMUS..............116
AIR-FRYER CRISPY CHICKPEAS..............117
HOMEMADE TRAIL MIX..............118
ROASTED BUFFALO CHICKPEAS..............119
AVOCADO HUMMUS..............120
BEET CHIPS..............121
BANANA ENERGY BITES..............122
DESSERT..............123
WINE-POACHED PEARS..............124
STRAWBERRIES WITH PEPPERED BALSAMIC DRIZZLE..............125
VANILLA CHIA SEED PUDDING WITH TOPPINGS..............126
MANGO BANANA SOFT SERVE..............127
30 DAYS MEAL PLAN..............129

Part One
The Overview

INTRODUCTION

Many people require medication to regulate their blood pressure. People with moderate hypertension may just require lifestyle modifications, such as switching to a better diet. However, for people who must take medicine to control their blood pressure, leading healthy lifestyles and eating well can help them take less medication overall. The heart must work harder to pump blood containing essential nutrients and oxygen throughout the body as a result of high blood pressure. The blood vessels' arteries thicken, get scarred, and lose their flexibility. Even while this process is a natural part of aging, those with high blood pressure experience it more quickly. The heart needs to work harder as the arteries stiffen, and the heart muscle becomes thicker, weaker, and less able to pump blood. High blood pressure can damage arteries, which can then affect the organs they serve. This kind of harm, for instance, can harm the heart, resulting in a heart attack, the brain, resulting in a stroke, or the kidneys, resulting in kidney failure. Your risk of getting high blood pressure (hypertension) is influenced by what you consume. According to research, high blood pressure can be avoided—Lowering salt consumption is part of the Dietary Approaches to Stop Hypertension (DASH) eating plan, which aims to prevent and treat hypertension. A blood pressure reading of 140/90 mmHg or greater is considered high. Prehypertension is defined as blood pressure between 120/80 and 139/89 millimeters of mercury (mmHg), which is the standard unit of measurement for blood pressure. But if you follow these recommendations, high blood pressure can be avoided and reduced.

- Follow a healthy dietary regimen that calls for low-sodium foods, such as DASH.
- Uphold a healthy weight.

Engage in light exercise for at least 2 hours and 30 minutes every week.

Scientists have developed specialized dietary methods to assist lower blood pressure because nutrition is known to play a significant impact in the development of high blood pressure. The DASH diet, which was created to help people manage high blood pressure and lower their risk of developing heart disease, is discussed in this book.

WHAT IS DASH DIET

Dietary Approaches to Stop Hypertension, or DASH diet, is a healthy eating strategy created to assist lower blood pressure and enhance overall health. The diet places an emphasis on consuming complete, nutrient-dense foods such fruits, vegetables, whole grains, lean proteins, and low-fat dairy products while avoiding those that are heavy in saturated and trans fats, added sugars, and sodium. It has been demonstrated that the DASH diet lowers blood pressure and lowers the risk of heart disease, stroke, and other illnesses. Additionally, it is a flexible and balanced diet that can be altered to accommodate different dietary needs and tastes.

Dash Diet Containing both fruits and vegetables

The diet was developed as a result of studies showing that those who ate a plant-based diet, such as vegans and vegetarians, had much lower rates of high blood pressure. Because of this, the DASH diet prioritizes fruits and vegetables while also including certain lean protein sources, such as chicken, fish, and legumes. Red meat, salt, added sugars, and fat are all restricted in the diet. The fact that this diet limits salt consumption, according to scientists, is one of the key reasons people with high blood pressure can benefit from it.

The standard DASH diet regimen recommends consuming no more sodium than 1 teaspoon (2,300 mg) per day, which is in accordance with the majority of national recommendations.

The version with less salt advises taking no more than 3/4 teaspoon (1,500 mg) of sodium each day. Fruits, vegetables, low-fat milk, whole grains, fish, chicken, legumes, and nuts are the foundation of the DASH diet. It advises cutting off red meat, added sugars in foods and beverages, and sodium. The diet is heart-healthy because it reduces the consumption of saturated and trans fats while boosting the consumption of potassium, magnesium, calcium, protein, and fiber—nutrients thought to help regulate blood pressure.

Adhering to the DASH Diet entails consuming a range of foods from different food groups that studies have shown to be good for heart health while avoiding others that have been proven to be unhealthy. Essential components include the following:

- Veggies and fruits
- Whole grain foods
- Legumes, seeds, and nuts
- Limit your intake of red and processed meat and focus on lean proteins like fish and chicken.
- Fat-free or low-fat dairy
- Avoid clear beverages with added sugar.
- Low salt—if kept to fewer than 2,300 mg per day, the diet is much more beneficial for lowering blood pressure, which can fall to even lower levels with less than 1,500 mg per day of sodium intake.
- Increased intake of dietary components such as fiber, calcium, magnesium, and potassium
- Saturated fat, trans fat, and cholesterol levels that are lower

The Dietary Approaches to Stopping Hypertension (DASH) Diet is based on two studies that examined strategies to lower blood pressure through dietary changes, DASH and DASH-Sodium. In the DASH study, participants were given one of three diets: the DASH diet, which is high in fruits, vegetables, and low-fat dairy products and low in saturated fat, total fat, and cholesterol. The other two diets were similar to the typical North American diet in terms of nutrients. The findings were convincing.

Both the DASH diet and the diet richer in fruits and vegetables lower blood pressure. Blood pressure was most significantly lowered by the DASH diet within two weeks of beginning the program.

Total cholesterol as well as low-density lipoprotein (LDL), or "bad cholesterol," were decreased in addition to blood pressure. Participants in the DASH-Sodium study were randomly assigned to one of three sodium regimens: the DASH diet with 3,300 mg of sodium per day (a normal amount for many North Americans); 2,300 mg of sodium; or 1,500 mg of sodium (a more restricted amount, equivalent to about 2/3 of a teaspoon of salt); or no sodium at all. Every person on the DASH diet experienced decreased blood pressure. However, people's blood pressure decreased more significantly the less salt they ate. The highest drop in blood pressure was seen in those who previously had high blood pressure.

Numerous studies demonstrate the DASH diet's numerous health advantages. DASH lowers blood pressure in those with high blood pressure as well as in people with normal blood pressure, even without reducing sodium intake, according to a body of reliable evidence. If salt intake is restricted to less than 2300 mg per day, and even more so with a 1500 mg sodium restriction, it can result in significant blood pressure decreases.

DASH has also been shown to lower serum uric acid levels in people with hyperuricemia, which puts them at risk for a painful inflammatory condition known as gout. This is in comparison to a standard American diet (e.g., high intake of red and processed meats, beverages sweetened with sugar, sweets, and refined grains).

DASH is best for enhancing all of these illnesses because persons with gout frequently also have high blood pressure and other cardiovascular diseases.

In a controlled 8-week trial, participants were randomly assigned to follow the DASH diet (low in total/saturated fat with whole grains, poultry, fish, nuts, fruits, and vegetables), a fruit and vegetable-rich diet (more fruits and vegetables than control diet but same amount of fat), or a control diet (the typical American diet, which is high in fat and cholesterol). The DASH diet was found to reduce cardiovascular risk. Based on the individuals' blood pressure and cholesterol readings before and after the diet intervention, the researchers calculated a 10-year reduction in risk for cardiovascular disease. Participants who followed the DASH or fruit/vegetable diets had a 10% lower risk than those who followed the control diet, although women and Black people exhibited the biggest advantages with a 13% and 14% risk reduction, respectively.

BRIEF HISTORY OF DASH DIET

In the US, high blood pressure is characterized as having a reading that is typically greater than 140/90 mmHg and affects one in three persons. The systolic pressure of blood against the arteries when the heart is contracting is represented by the top number, 140. The diastolic pressure in the arteries during rest or between heartbeats is represented by the bottom number, 90. The risk of heart disease, renal disease, and stroke increases with blood pressure, which is cause for alarm. Since high blood pressure has no symptoms or warning indications, it is referred to as the silent killer.

The National Heart, Lung, and Blood Institute's (NHLBI) DASH research was the first to examine the impact of a diet high in potassium, magnesium, and calcium—rather than supplements—on blood pressure. It was published in the New England Journal of Medicine in 1977; 459 adults with and without high blood pressure participated in the study.

Blood pressure levels needed to be between 80 and 95 mmHg for diastole and less than 160 mmHg for systole. 60% of the participants were African Americans, and around half of them were women. Three diets were contrasted. The first had a high fat content (37% of calories) and little fruit and vegetables, much like the usual American diet. The American diet was the second option, although it included more fruits and vegetables. The third diet had a high fruit and vegetable content, low-fat dairy products, and overall low fat content (less than 30% of calories). Per 2,000 calories, it also offered 1,240 mg calcium, 500 mg magnesium, and 4,700 mg potassium. The DASH diet is now referred to as this. Each of the three regimens had the same amount of sodium, or 7 grams (g) of salt, or around 3,000 mg of sodium per day. This was close to the current salt intake guidelines of 4-5 g per day and about 20% less than the average adult intake in the United States. Each person's calorie intake was modified to maintain weight. To rule out salt restriction and weight loss as probable causes for any changes in blood pressure, these two parameters were added. To improve adherence to the diets, all of the participants' meals were prepared in one large kitchen.

The DASH regimen was the most successful, according to the results, although eating more fruits and vegetables also had a lowering effect. It decreased systolic pressure by 6 mmHg and diastolic pressure by 3 mmHg in subjects without high blood pressure. Participants with high blood pressure had better outcomes; their systolic and diastolic pressures dropped by almost twice as much, to 11 and 6 mmHg, respectively. These findings demonstrated that the DASH diet appeared to drop blood pressure in a manner comparable to that found with the use of a single blood pressure medication, as well as a diet that restricted salt intake to 3 grams. The DASH plan's effects, which are equivalent to drug treatment, were felt after two weeks of beginning it and persisted throughout the course of the experiment. This trial offered the first scientific proof that dietary components other than sodium alone, such as potassium, calcium, and magnesium, had a significant impact on blood pressure.

MEDICAL SPECIALIZATIONS

In the 1990s, the DASH diet—an acronym for Dietary Approaches to Stop Hypertension—was created as a dietary strategy to lower hypertension combined with a decrease in dietary salt. The Mediterranean diet, which encourages a diet high in fruits and vegetables, low-fat dairy products, soluble dietary fiber, whole grains, and plant-based protein while being low in saturated fatty acids, serves as the main inspiration for this diet.

The authors draw attention to the high potassium content of this diet. The DASH diet is endorsed by the American Heart Association and is widely acknowledged by medical professionals as a useful method of controlling blood pressure. Thus, the DASH diet considerably lowers systolic and diastolic blood pressure in both hypertensive and normotensive individuals (by 11 and 5 mmHg, respectively), compared to a control diet, whose daily dose of table salt is already decreased to 8 grams. The DASH diet is today regarded as one of the best diets for sustaining good health, in accordance with the recommendations of public health authorities, in addition to its effects on cardiovascular health.

The MIND diet was created by the team of Martha Claire Morris, who released the initial findings in 2015. The moniker MIND, an acronym for Mediterranean-DASH Intervention for Neurodegenerative Delay, refers to a diet that is likewise based on the principles of the Mediterranean diet and builds on the DASH diet by providing a prominent place to items and ingredients that may enhance brain health. Green vegetables (spinach, lettuce, green beans) and other vegetables, nuts (walnuts, hazelnuts, almonds), berries (raspberries, currants, blueberries), dried beans, whole grains, fish and poultry (occasionally), olive oil, and even wine—in moderation—are among the ten foods recommended by the MIND diet. On the other hand, this approach suggests limiting the consumption of five food categories: red meats, butter and fatty cheeses, pastries, and fried meals. It is therefore advised not to eat more than four portions of red meat or even five pastries per week, which is a limitation but not a ban.

This gives one some latitude to sample their preferred meals without getting too frustrated.

Both for sustaining good mental health and as a method of preserving good general health, this MIND diet exhibits some encouraging results. To confirm the beneficial effects of this diet with greater assurance, large-scale, long-term research will be required.

The DASH and MIND diets, like the Mediterranean diet, are very simple to follow and have lower dropout rates than diets that are more restrictive or demand significant behavioral adjustments.

There are no nutrient categories that are prohibited by the DASH, MIND, or Mediterranean diets. They approach international nutritional requirements by recommending various sources and adjusting the ratios.

Therefore, unlike other diets that promote or strongly restrict one of the groups, these diets always allow for starchy meals (carbohydrates that are broken down into sugars), proteins, and lipids. Thus, the proportion of starches and lipids in the Dukan and Atkins diets was dramatically reduced in favor of proteins, while the Paleolithic diet severely limited carbs in favor of lipids and proteins. Although such imbalances can have positive short-term impacts, particularly on weight loss, the scientific community strongly doubts their long-term implications.

THE MEDITERRANEAN DIET AND THE DASH DIET SHARE FIVE GUIDING PRINCIPLES

The main principles of the Mediterranean diet serve as inspiration for other DASH diet principles. Let's start by pointing out that both lead to a simpler, healthier, and more diversified diet.

1 -- Fruits and vegetables at the heart of the diet

Consuming foods that are naturally low in sodium, or favoring fresh fruits and vegetables, is one of the tenets of the DASH diet. They also serve as our primary supply of fiber and are a good source of vitamins, minerals, trace elements, and antioxidants, which is a plus.

Also worth remembering is the superior design of nature. The reason why fruits and vegetables are in season is that they give us the nutrients we require at the appropriate time. For example, the bulk of summertime fruits and vegetables are mostly water to help us stay hydrated throughout the dry and hot weather.

How about in terms of volume? The Mediterranean diet advises eating a serving of vegetables with each meal. The DASH diet presents a greater challenge because everything depends on calorie intake and profile. However, the amount varies daily between 300 and 400 g (80 to 100 g is about similar to one portion). that is, three to four pieces each day.

2 -- No to processed products

As we've seen, one of the DASH diet's tenets is to limit foods that are heavy in sodium, oil, and saturated sugars. To limit intake of prepared meals, processed foods, and fried foods in particular.

In order to benefit from fresh, uncooked foods, the DASH diet emphasizes them more than the Mediterranean diet does. The DASH diet is a return to the fundamentals. To concentrate on the best components of the other food groups (including fruits and vegetables), remove the extraneous ingredients from prepared meals.

3 -- More legumes, dried fruits and whole grains on the menu

Regarding additional food groups, here are three that are becoming less and less common in our kitchens but still play a role in these two diets: legumes (like chickpeas and lentils), dry fruits (like pecans and walnuts), and whole grains (like whole wheat pasta or even quinoa, brown rice, and corn).

Including them in our diets not only adds diversity but also offers their beneficial nutrients. Additionally, by combining legumes and whole grains, we can increase our intake of protein while decreasing our consumption of animal proteins, particularly red meat. Additionally, this combo offers fiber and complex carbohydrates.

4 -- Less salt and more spices to cook differently

In the modern kitchen, salt is widely used. It replaces the primary (or even special) taste enhancer. It is not the only component that can fulfill this function, though. Mediterranean's use spices, herbs, and garden herbs in their daily cooking. They provide the food flavor and make it possible to change up the recipes. If the same pan-fried vegetables are prepared with basil, coriander, mint, saffron, or turmeric, they will have various fragrances, benefits, and flavors. The aim is to cook differently whether you choose to follow the DASH diet or the Mediterranean diet. cooking with different condiments once more. Use fresh or dried herbs and spices, as well as garlic, onion, and less salt.

5 -- Regular physical activity

The DASH diet also suggests engaging in regular physical activity. The idea is not necessarily to go into a sport or to do it intensely, like in Mediterranean culture. Simply go for a stroll, swim, or get some fresh air. It's important to move. Speaking of basics, other key components of the Mediterranean diet include laughing, grinning, taking deep breaths, and appreciating the surroundings. Because the Mediterranean diet teaches us how to live well, whereas the DASH diet teaches us the fundamentals of (excellent) nutrition!

THE HEALTH BENEFITS OF THE DASH DIET

The DASH diet is a whole foods regimen that emphasizes the consumption of fresh produce, whole grains, legumes, nuts, low-fat dairy products, fish, and chicken. Being naturally low in sodium, refined sugar, and saturated and trans fats, it is regarded as a heart-healthy diet. It improves the intake of fiber, antioxidants, potassium, magnesium, calcium, and other nutrients that are crucial for cardiovascular health. The DASH diet and continued physical activity will have the biggest impact on decreasing blood pressure and some other benefit to the health system which include Reduce High Blood Pressure.

Blood arteries experience pressure when blood flows through them, and this pressure is measured as blood pressure. Systolic pressure over diastolic pressure, or 120/80 mmHg, is how blood pressure is measured in millimeters of mercury (mmHg). The top number, or systolic blood pressure, represents the pressure in the veins when the heart beats. The pressure in the vessels while the heart is not beating is known as diastolic blood pressure, which is represented by the bottom number.

Following are the categories used by the American College of Cardiology to categorize blood pressure:

·More than 120/80 mmHg is abnormal.

·Diastolic less than 80 mmHg and systolic 120-129 mmHg are considered elevated.

·Systolic 130-139 mmHg or diastolic 80-89 mmHg is stage 1 hypertension.

·Systolic 140 mmHg or diastolic 90 mmHg is considered stage 2 hypertension.

·Systolic pressure of 180 mmHg or higher and/or a diastolic pressure of 120 mmHg constitute a hypertensive crisis.

Systolic pressure: The force exerted by your heartbeat on your blood vessels.

Diastolic pressure: When your heart is at rest, this is the pressure in your blood arteries between beats.

Blood pressure increases can also be caused by genes and stress. Your doctor can occasionally be unable to pinpoint a specific cause for your high blood pressure. What is described as essential hypertension is that. When your doctor discusses your blood pressure with you, he is talking to the force that your blood exerts on the artery walls. Your systolic blood pressure is the highest reading on the scale. That pressure is the result of your heart's pumping action on your blood vessels. The diastolic blood pressure, which is shown by the lower figure, is the pressure experienced while your heart is at rest in between beats. Your blood pressure should remain 120 over 80 or below. High blood pressure is defined as 140 over 90 or higher.

You might wonder why high blood pressure is a concern. High blood pressure might be compared to a river that is flowing too quickly; eventually, the banks will be damaged. When you have high blood pressure, your artery walls gradually become damaged due to the additional pressure your blood exerts on them. Additionally, it can harm your kidneys, heart, and other organs. How can you determine if you have high blood pressure, then? Because high blood pressure frequently lacks signs like a fever or a cough, you may not even be aware of it. The majority of the time, high blood pressure has no symptoms at all, and you won't know you have it unless you've had it checked or you've experienced complications like heart disease or renal issues. You can use a home blood pressure monitor to check it yourself, or you can visit your doctor to have it done. If it's high, you'll decide on a blood pressure target with your doctor. You can accomplish that objective by following a balanced diet, doing out for at least 30 minutes each day, giving up smoking, consuming less than 1,500 milligrams of salt each day, and employing stress-relieving techniques like yoga and meditation. If, however, these lifestyle modifications are insufficient to control your blood pressure, your doctor may recommend one or more medications.

Because uncontrolled blood pressure can lead to a number of significant health issues, including as heart attack, stroke, renal disease, and eyesight loss, doctors take their patients' blood pressure very seriously. It's better to take control of your blood pressure by being proactive.

The DASH diet has its roots in the 1990s, when the NIH supported multiple research to identify a therapeutic diet that was successful in treating high blood pressure. They came to the conclusion that blood pressure might be lowered by the DASH diet without weight reduction or purposeful sodium restriction. Blood pressure reductions can be amplified by using the DASH diet in conjunction with sodium control and weight loss.

REDUCE HIGH CHOLESTEROL

What is cholesterol?

A lipid (fat) called cholesterol is produced by the liver and is present in many of the foods we consume. Cholesterol is necessary for good health because it performs various crucial tasks for the efficient operation of your body.

- The membranes of your cells absorb about 90% of the cholesterol in your body.
- It functions as a component of specific sex hormones (testosterone) or adrenal hormones (cortisone).
- It controls how specific fetal cells develop.
- It encourages the development of synapses in the brain.
- It is a component of bile, a fluid that digests dietary fats by combining lipids and water.
- It is a form of vitamin D.

LDL (Low Density Lipoprotein), a low-density protein, and HDL (High Density Lipoprotein), a high-density lipoprotein, are two types of "lipoproteins" that transport cholesterol in the blood. The terms "total cholesterol" refer to both HDL and LDL cholesterol, also known as good (HDL) and bad (LDL) cholesterol.

The good cholesterol: When cholesterol builds up in the arteries, HDL lipoproteins pick it up and carry it to the liver, where it is excreted. Poor-quality fatty deposits are removed from the arteries by HDL cholesterol. HDL binds 20–30% of blood cholesterol.

Bad cholesterol: LDL lipoproteins, which are bad for the body, bind cholesterol to the artery walls and cause atherosclerotic plaques to develop. Since LDL makes up 60 to 80% of the cholesterol in the blood, it has a tendency to clog the arteries.

It is a necessary component not only for the construction of the membrane that envelops the cells but also for the manufacture of several hormones. Although high cholesterol is a risk factor for various heart and blood vessel illnesses, it is not a disease in and of itself. After numerous years of having too much cholesterol, the arteries gradually lose their flexibility, which reduces their diameter. This condition is known as atherosclerosis (also known as arteriosclerosis), a condition with potentially harmful effects. The treatment of excess cholesterol is based on dietary measures and specific medications. Although high cholesterol is a risk factor for various heart and blood vessel illnesses, it is not a disease in and of itself. In actuality, an excess of LDL cholesterol, often known as bad cholesterol, encourages the development of deposits on the artery walls. These buildups gradually limit the diameter of the arteries and induce a loss of flexibility in the arteries, which raises the risk of infarction, stroke, or arteritis.

Effect and Symptoms of High Cholesterol

Although high LDL cholesterol does not directly result in disease, its buildup in the arteries can. For instance, myocardial infarction, angina pectoris, or even a heart artery contraction. Paralysis, vertigo, linguistic difficulties, and even a stroke may result from clogged brain arteries. Arteritis results in sporadic calf cramps during walking if the arteries in the legs are restricted. Additionally, erectile dysfunction is noted.

How Dash Diet Reduce High Cholesterol

The DASH diet includes a number of elements that have been shown to lower cholesterol levels, including eating a lot of fiber (which comes from fruits, vegetables, whole grains, nuts, and legumes), eating fish and leaner meat cuts, and avoiding sugar and refined carbohydrates.

However, the DASH diet also causes a reduction in HDL ("good") cholesterol. The DASH diet is helpful at lowering markers of LDL and VLDL ("bad") cholesterol and triglycerides. Further studies have revealed that a higher fat DASH diet, which replaces 10% of the total daily calories from carbohydrates with unsaturated fat, is equally as effective at lowering blood pressure, LDL cholesterol, and triglycerides without causing unintended decreases in HDL cholesterol.

Reduce Cardiovascular Diseases

Heart and blood vessel illnesses are collectively referred to as cardiovascular diseases. These conditions may impact a single or multiple areas of your heart and/or blood vessels. A person may have symptoms (physical manifestations of the disease) or be asymptomatic (complete lack of symptoms).

Cardiovascular disease encompasses problems with the heart or blood vessels, such as:

- Narrowing of the blood arteries in your body, whether it be in your heart, other organs, or elsewhere.
- Birth defects in the heart and blood vessels are evident.
- improperly functioning heart valves.
- abnormal heartbeats.

Depending on the exact form, cardiovascular disease can have a variety of causes. For instance, coronary artery disease and peripheral artery disease are brought on by atherosclerosis (plaque buildup in your arteries). Arrhythmias can be brought on by coronary artery disease, cardiac muscle scarring, genetic issues, or drug side effects. Valve problems can be brought on by aging, infections, an improper diet, and rheumatic disease.

What are the risk factors for cardiovascular disease?

If you have risk factors like these, you could be more prone to develop cardiovascular disease:

- Hypertension is a term for high blood pressure.
- Hyperlipidemia, or high cholesterol.
- Use of tobacco, including vaping.
- Diabetes type 2.
- Heart disease in the family history.
- Absence of exercise.
- Being overweight or obese.
- Diet high in sodium, sugar and fat.
- Alcoholism in excess.
- Use of illegal or prescription drugs.
- Gestational diabetes.
- Chronic inflammatory or autoimmune conditions.
- Chronic kidney disease.

Depending on the reason, cardiovascular disease symptoms can change. More modest symptoms may be seen in older folks and those who were born assigned as females. They are still susceptible to major cardiovascular disease, though.

Signs of a cardiac condition:

- Angina, or chest pain.
- Pressure, weight, or discomfort in the chest that has been compared to a "belt around the chest" or a "weight on the chest."
- Dyspnea, or shortness of breath.
- fainting or dizziness.
- weariness or fatigue.

How Dash Diet Reduce Cardiovascular Diseases

Adopting the DASH (Dietary Approaches to Stop Hypertension) diet may have the biggest impact on young and middle-aged persons among numerous lifestyle changes that may lower cardiovascular disease. Over the next ten years, researchers predict that broad adoption of lifestyle modifications, such as avoiding excessive alcohol intake and engaging in regular exercise, might avert thousands of deaths and save more than $1 billion in medical expenses. According to their findings, following the DASH diet could be most advantageous.

The DASH diet is especially created to assist in controlling blood pressure.

The diet places a strong emphasis on foods including fruits, vegetables, lean meat sources, nuts, seeds, and whole grains while restricting the consumption of red meat, sodium, sweets, and beverages with added sugar.

The majority of cardiovascular disorders, such as heart attack and stroke, are significantly influenced by hypertension. The DASH diet can effectively lower and normalize blood pressure, which can dramatically reduce the risk of cardiovascular disease by 20%. It is specifically linked to a 29% lower risk of heart failure and a 19% lower risk of stroke.

WEIGHT LOSS

The DASH diet is an effective option for managing weight, especially for those who are overweight or obese. According to a recent meta-analysis, persons who followed the DASH diet for 24 weeks lost more weight than those who followed a calorie-restricted conventional American diet.

Whether or not you lose weight while following the DASH diet, you'll probably have decreased blood pressure. However, it's likely that you have received advice to decrease weight if you already have high blood pressure.

This is because your blood pressure is more likely to be greater the more weight you have.

Additionally, it has been demonstrated that decreasing weight can lower blood pressure. According to certain research, the DASH diet can help people lose weight. Those who have lost weight on the DASH diet, on the other hand, have done so while maintaining a regulated calorie deficit, which means they were instructed to consume fewer calories than they were burning. People may discover that they automatically cut back on their calorie consumption and lose weight when following the DASH diet since it excludes so many high-fat, sugary meals. Others might need to consciously limit their intake. In either case, you'll still need to follow a calorie-reduced diet if you wish to lose weight while following the DASH diet. DASH has proven to work. If you want to lose weight, DASH won't help you do so quickly. However, it is possible to lose weight and improve your health at the same time if you choose the right calorie amount and keep to it consistently.

There are numerous free web resources available to get assistance because DASH has been used for so long and is widely regarded by medical professionals.

Enhance the Metabolic Syndrome

High blood pressure, high blood sugar, abdominal obesity, low HDL cholesterol, and high triglycerides are at least three of the symptoms of metabolic syndrome. The DASH diet can help manage and prevent metabolic syndrome by enhancing these indicators.

Reduce Type 2 Diabetes

A 20% risk decrease in developing type 2 diabetes in the future is linked to the DASH diet. Diabetes type 2 and prediabetes are preceded by insulin resistance, which is the body's desensitization to insulin and the rise in blood sugar that results. The DASH diet successfully raises insulin sensitivity, especially when used in conjunction with a complete program for lifestyle modification that involves exercise and weight loss. Weirdly, both high- and low-GI DASH diets had the same effects on insulin sensitivity, suggesting that using the glycemic index (GI) to choose foods high in carbohydrates is not necessary.

Lower Your Gout Risk

DASH can lower serum uric acid levels in comparison to a Standard American Diet, which reduces the risk of gout. The DASH diet would be beneficial in treating all problems given that it is widely believed that gout is a metabolic disease that frequently co-occurs with high blood pressure and other cardiovascular disorders.

Improve Kidney Health

A lower risk of kidney disease is linked to DASH dietary patterns, which include consuming less red meat and processed food and more nuts, legumes, and low-fat dairy products. The DASH diet's high consumption of calcium, phytates, magnesium, and citrate is linked to a lower incidence of kidney stones, as does consuming fruits and vegetables.

THE DASH DIET FOOD

Similar to the well-known Mediterranean diet, the Dash diet prioritizes "good" fats, lean animal proteins, water, soluble and insoluble fibers, vitamins, minerals, antioxidants (flavonoids, polyphenols...), and vegetable proteins. Specifically, humans ingest 27% fats, 18% proteins, and 55% carbohydrates everyday.

Here are some reminders to "eat Dash" without making your life more difficult:

- We eat 5 portions of 80 g each of fresh or frozen fruits and vegetables, without added sugar, at the rate of 3 fruits and 2 vegetables each day.
- We eat a portion of meat, an egg, fish, seafood, tofu, or a vegetarian steak every day at noon and in the evening.
- We eat a little amount of potatoes, whole grains, or other starchy foods at every meal.
- We consume a minimum of 1 liter of water every day, or 75% water and 25% tea or herbal tea.

The best Dash foods are thus:

1.Garlic: This detox food boosts the immune system's function and helps maintain a healthy balance of intestinal flora in addition to being great for the heart (anti-cholesterol, anti-hypertension, etc.). Additionally, it has a healthy amount of prebiotic fibers (1 gram for 2 raw pods) that nourish the "good" bacteria that live in our intestines.

2.Berries: Blueberries, blackberries, currants, blackcurrants, and other small red and black fruits are extremely low in calories and sugar; these are without a doubt the greatest "Dash" fruits because they are also extremely concentrated in vitamins, minerals, and antioxidants.

3.Broccoli: For the liver, intestinal flora, heart, brain, and immunity, broccoli is a fantastic source of vitamin C, calcium, and protective phytochemicals. This is true of all cabbages: It must be, whether it is uncooked, cooked, fresh, or frozen.

4.Turmeric: A super-joke from Dash: Turmeric lowers cholesterol and reduces inflammation. Additionally, it treats intestinal issues with nearly no calories.

5.Sardines: Sardines, like all fish, are a great option for a Dash plate that is well-balanced. It also has a good amount of vitamin D and omega-3 fatty acids without being overly polluted.

FRUIT

4 to 5 servings are recommended per day.

The DASH diet permits the consumption of all fruits. In fact, it encourages their consumption, dismissing concerns about the natural sugars in fruits being unhealthy. Enjoy 4 to 5 servings daily, incorporating them into desserts, toppings, smoothies, and snacks. Each person should be served with just 1/2 cup of fresh fruit and 1/4 cup of dried fruit. Here's a revised list of fruit examples: Apples, Blueberries, Grapes, Kiwi, Oranges, Raspberries, Banana, Peach, Pear, Nectarine, Plum, Cherries, Berries, Mango, Pineapple, Melon Strawberries

LOW-FAT DAIRY PRODUCTS

2-3 servings every day.

Replace your full-fat dairy products with low-fat or fat-free options since the diet advises avoiding foods high in saturated fat. However, you can still have 2 to 3 servings of dairy products daily, as long as they are low in fat and sodium. Here's a revised list of dairy products: Cheese, Eggs, Low fat yogurt, Milk, Yogurt

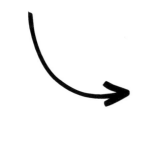

HIGH-SODIUM FOODS

4 to 5 servings are recommended per day.
The DASH diet permits the consumption of all fruits. In fact, consuming them is encouraged by the diet. Get over your concern that fruit's inherent sugars are unhealthy. Enjoy 4 to 5 servings daily in the form of dessert, toppings, smoothies, and snacks. Just 1/2 cup of fresh fruit and 1/4 cup of dried fruit should be served per person.
Apples, Blueberries, Grapes, Kiwi, Oranges, Raspberries, Banana, Peach, Pear, Nectarine, Plum, Cherries, Berries, Mango, Pineapple, Melon Strawberries

LEAN PROTEINS

Although the vegetarian lifestyle served as the inspiration for the DASH diet, it is not entirely plant-based. A maximum of 6 ounces of lean meat or eggs may be consumed per day. Although it may not seem like much, persons with hypertension and heart health issues may benefit from eating less meat. Steer clear of frying and stick to poultry and fish. Tofu and tempeh are options for vegetarians and vegans.
Chicken, oily fish, Herrings, Mackerel, Salmon, Sardines,
Tuna, lean beef, Turkey

VEGETABLES

5 to 6 servings should be consumed daily. Vegetables are a beloved food category for many people. As you age, vegetables become even more appealing. The DASH diet recommends consuming five to six servings of vegetables per day. Don't be afraid to explore new vegetables like spaghetti squash, but also consider using familiar favorites like peas and carrots in soups, salads, and side dishes.

Here is a list of vegetables that you can incorporate into your diet: chickpeas, black beans, black-eyed peas, red beans, potatoes, sweet potatoes, avocados, peppers, carrots, cucumbers, garlic, kale, lettuce, onions, seeds, chia seeds, flaxseed, pumpkin, sunflower, spinach, tomatoes, and zucchini

GRAINS AND STARCHY FOODS

Servings per day: 6 to 8
The DASH diet emphasizes the consumption of whole grains due to their ability to lower the risk of hypertension, with a recommended intake of 6 to 8 servings per day. While it may seem complicated, incorporating whole grains into your diet can be as simple as having whole grain cereal or oatmeal for breakfast, and choosing options like quinoa, brown rice, or whole wheat pasta for lunch and dinner.

Here is a list of foods that fall under the category of whole grains: sliced bread, tortillas, rolls, bagels, crackers (low sodium), dry cereal and granola, rice, pasta, quinoa, oats, grits, polenta, barley, couscous, ancient grains, sprouted grains, corn, lima beans, and yams

NUTS, SEEDS, BEANS, AND LEGUMES

4-5 servings each week.

This food group should be consumed four to five times per week, according to the DASH Diet. While legumes like beans and lentils are fantastic sources of plant protein and high in fiber, nuts and seeds are excellent sources of healthful fats. These high-fiber meals will help you increase your fiber intake, which is a key component of the DASH diet. All of these foods are rich in essential vitamins and minerals. However, due to their higher calorie content, the recommended servings for these food groups are fewer compared to other dietary groups.

Almonds (unsalted), Pistachios (unsalted), Cashews (unsalted), Walnuts (unsalted), Peanuts (unsalted), Peanut Butter, Almond Butter, Tahini, Chia Seeds, Flax Seeds, Hemp Seeds, Sunflower Seeds, Sesame Seeds, Green Beans, Lentils

HEART-HEALTHY OILS

Servings: two to three per day

The Mediterranean diet, which is rich in healthful fats, served as inspiration for some aspects of the DASH diet. The DASH diet includes heart-healthy fats as well, which is why adherents eat 2 to 3 servings of monounsaturated fats daily. Olive oil will probably be your go-to oil.

- Olive oil
- Canola oil
- Safflower oil
- Low-fat mayonnaise

LOW FAT SWEETS

Although the designers of the DASH diet are aware that occasionally you'll want to reward yourself, it better to limit your consumption of sweets. In such situations, they have provided a list of sweets that are acceptable to consume five times a week or less.
The DASH diet endorses low-fat desserts include:
- Fruit-flavored gelatin
- Jelly
- Maple syrup
- Sorbet and ices

Seeds/cereals: Brown rice, Buckwheat, Bulgur, couscous, Pearl barley, Wholemeal pasta, Whole wheat bread

Foods and drinks to be avoided while following a DASH diet
The DASH diet is a balanced eating plan that does not eliminate any food groups, so it is not particularly novel. The DASH diet promotes the consumption of simple, natural foods that are free from chemical and industrial ingredients as much as possible. It shares similarities with the Mediterranean, Okinawa, and GI diets

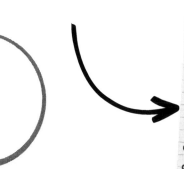

RED MEATS

The DASH diet prioritizes fish and poultry over red meat, according to research conducted in 1999. Red meat consumption should be limited, although it is not technically forbidden, due to its high content of saturated fat and cholesterol. Red meats include:
- beef
- pork
- lamb
- veal

SATURATED FAT

There is conflicting data regarding the connection between saturated fat and heart disease; however, the DASH diet takes a cautious approach and advises reducing the consumption of foods high in saturated fat.
- Cheese
- Fatty cuts of meat
- Poultry with skin
- Lard
- Cream
- Butter
- Whole milk

ADDED SUGAR

You should become accustomed to reading the ingredient lists on packaged foods if you follow the DASH diet and avoid adding sugar cubes to your tea. Despite the limited research on sugar and hypertension, some data suggest that sugar may raise blood pressure. Even if there may not be a clear connection between the two, it is still advisable to limit added sugar because it is calorie-dense without providing any nutritional benefits.
- Table sugar
- Sweets
- Condiments with added sugar
- Junk food

You eat moderate portions of:
- Fat-free or low-fat dairy products. ·Whole grains. Lean meats, poultry, beans, soy foods, legumes, and eggs or egg substitutes
- Fish
- ·Nuts and seeds
- Heart-healthy fats, such as olive oil, canola oil, or avocados

FREQUENTLY ASKED QUESTIONS

QUESTION: Can Dash diet be vegetarian?

The DASH diet could easily be a vegetarian diet if legumes (for example, beans, lentils, peas, and peanuts) were substituted for meat. Vegetarian diets tend to be higher in potassium, magnesium, and calcium, as does the DASH diet. Vegetarian diets also are higher in fiber and unsaturated fats than other diets.

QUESTION: I can't tolerate lactose or am allergic to dairy. Can I still follow the DASH diet?

Yogurt, most cheeses, and warm milk products can all be consumed by lactose intolerant individuals in large quantities. Since nonfat milk still includes lactose, not sure why so many people can tolerate it. Additionally, some people who are allergic to or intolerant to milk proteins can consume yogurt or cheese. You can also use dairy alternatives like soy or rice milk, yogurt, or cheeses, as long as they have the same amounts of calcium and vitamin D as the original items. For those who are sensitive to the protein in cow's milk, goat milk is an additional option.

QUESTION: Is the DASH diet high fiber and low fat?

Yes, the DASH diet has a high fiber content and has little to no fat, most of which are heart-healthy fats. Extremely low-fat diets are linked to increased appetite, which is detrimental when trying to establish and maintain a balanced eating routine.

QUESTION: Is sea salt preferable to table salt for lowering sodium levels?

Although many varieties of sea salt have a little less sodium than ordinary salt, they can nevertheless contribute to high dietary sodium levels.

Additionally, sea salt frequently has smaller granules with higher weights (and sodium) per teaspoon. Instead of trying to rely just on adding salt to dishes to impart flavor, it is tremendously beneficial to learn various methods of seasoning. We encourage cooking with little to no extra salt in the DASH Diet Cookbook as well as in all of the recipes.

QUESTION: Can sweeteners be used in the DASH diet?

In the DASH diet, there is no specific mention of the use of artificial sweeteners. While artificial sweeteners can provide a low-calorie alternative for sweetening foods and beverages, it is important to consider that excessive use of artificial sweeteners may impact taste preferences for natural flavors. Additionally, some research suggests that excessive use of artificial sweeteners may be associated with metabolic issues and other health complications.

If you need to sweeten foods or beverages in the DASH diet, it is preferable to opt for more natural options such as fresh fruit, honey, or small amounts of cane sugar.

QUESTION: Is it recommended to skip breakfast?

No, it is not recommended to skip breakfast on the DASH diet. Breakfast is considered an important meal and an integral part of a healthy lifestyle.

Skipping breakfast may lead to feelings of hunger and a higher likelihood of making less healthy food choices throughout the rest of the day. Therefore, it is advisable to have a balanced breakfast as part of a healthy lifestyle based on the DASH diet.

QUESTION: What is the recommended duration for following the DASH diet?

The recommended duration for following the DASH diet depends on individual needs and goals. In general, the DASH diet is designed as a long-term dietary approach rather than a temporary diet. However, every individual is different, so it is always advisable to consult a healthcare professional or a dietitian to obtain personalized guidance on the duration and adaptation of the DASH diet based on your specific needs and goals.

QUESTION: What can I do to prepare adequately before starting this diet?

Before starting the diet, you can prepare by educating yourself about the principles and guidelines of the DASH diet, stocking up on nutritious foods, and planning your meals and snacks in advance.

QUESTION: What are the tips for staying motivated and overcoming any challenges during this diet?

To stay motivated during the DASH diet, set realistic goals, track your progress, seek support from friends or family, find enjoyable ways to stay physically active, and remind yourself of the health benefits you will gain from following the diet.

QUESTION: What are the success strategies reported by others who have followed this diet?

Certain tactics for success have been shared by people who have followed the DASH diet. These include introducing dietary changes gradually, prioritizing whole and unprocessed foods, practicing portion control, decreasing sodium intake, and seeking personalized advice from healthcare professionals or registered dietitians. Please be aware that these responses are concise, and for more comprehensive information, it is advisable to consult a healthcare professional or registered dietitian.

Part Two
The Recipes

Breakfast

BERRY-ALMOND SMOOTHIE BOWL

INGREDIENTS

- ⅔ cup frozen raspberries
- ½ cup frozen sliced banana
- ½ cup plain unsweetened almond milk
- 5 tablespoons sliced almonds, divided
- ¼ teaspoon ground cinnamon
- ⅛ teaspoon ground cardamom
- ⅛ teaspoon vanilla extract
- ¼ cup blueberries
- 1 tablespoon unsweetened coconut flakes

PREPARATION

1. Blend the following ingredients in a blender: raspberries, banana, almond milk, 3 tablespoons almonds, cinnamon, cardamom, and vanilla. Blend until extremely smooth.
2. The remaining 2 tablespoons of almonds, 2 tablespoons of coconut, and blueberries should be added to the smoothie before serving.

Calories: 360
Fat: 7g
Carbs: 16g
Protein: 9g

SPINACH & EGG SCRAMBLE WITH RASPBERRIES

INGREDIENTS

- 1 teaspoon canola oil
- 1 ½ cups baby spinach (1 1/2 ounces)
- 2 large eggs, lightly beaten
- Pinch of kosher salt
- Pinch of ground pepper
- 1 slice whole-grain bread, toasted
- ½ cup fresh raspberries

PREPARATION

1. Heat oil in a small nonstick skillet over medium-high heat.
2. Add the spinach and simmer for 1 to 2 minutes, stirring frequently, until wilted. Onto a platter, transfer the spinach. Clean the pan, then add eggs and cook it up over medium-low.
3. Cook for 1 to 2 minutes, stirring once or twice to ensure even cooking.
4. Add the spinach, salt, and pepper, and stir.
5. Along with bread and strawberries, serve the scramble.

Calories: 296
Fat: 7g
Carbs: 21g
Protein: 10g

PINEAPPLE GREEN SMOOTHIE

INGREDIENTS

- ½ cup unsweetened almond milk
- ⅓ cup nonfat plain Greek yogurt
- 1 cup baby spinach
- 1 cup frozen banana slices (about 1 medium banana)
- ½ cup frozen pineapple chunks
- 1 tablespoon chia seeds
- 1-2 teaspoons pure maple syrup or honey (optional)

PREPARATION

1. Add almond milk and yogurt to a blender, then add spinach, banana, pineapple, chia seeds and sweetener (if using)
2. Blend until smooth.

Calories: 146
Fat: 2g
Carbs: 12g
Protein: 6g

CHOCOLATE-BANANA PROTEIN SMOOTHIE

1 SERVING

DIFFICULT

COST

INGREDIENTS

- 1 banana, frozen
- ½ cup cooked red lentils
- ½ cup nonfat milk
- 2 teaspoons unsweetened cocoa powder
- 1 teaspoon pure maple syrup

PREPARATION

1. Combine banana, lentils, milk, cocoa and syrup in a blender. Puree until smooth.

Calories: 310
Fat: 9
Carbs: 23g
Protein: 12g

RASPBERRY YOGURT CEREAL BOWL

INGREDIENTS

- 1 cup nonfat plain yogurt
- ½ cup mini shredded-wheat cereal
- ¼ cup fresh raspberries
- 2 teaspoons mini chocolate chips
- 1 teaspoon pumpkin seeds
- ¼ teaspoon ground cinnamon

PREPARATION

1. Place yogurt in a bowl and top with shredded wheat, raspberries, chocolate chips, pumpkin seeds and cinnamon.

Calories: 290
Fat: 5g
Carbs: 22g
Protein: 12g

SPINACH & EGG TACOS

INGREDIENTS

- ¼ avocado
- 1 teaspoon lime juice
- 2 hard-boiled eggs, chopped
- 2 corn tortillas, warmed
- 1 cup chopped spinach, divided
- 2 tablespoons shredded Cheddar cheese, divided
- 2 tablespoons salsa, divided

PREPARATION

1. Smash avocado in a small bowl with lime juice and salt.
2. Mix in eggs.
3. Divide the mixture between tortillas and top each with 1/2 cup spinach and 1 tablespoon each cheese and salsa.

Calories: 421
Fat: 14g
Carbs: 32g
Protein: 14g

REALLY GREEN SMOOTHIE

1 SERVING

DIFFICULT

COST

INGREDIENTS

- ¼ avocado
- 1 teaspoon lime juice
- 2 hard-boiled eggs, chopped
- 2 corn tortillas, warmed
- 1 cup chopped spinach, divided
- 2 tablespoons shredded Cheddar cheese, divided
- 2 tablespoons salsa, divided

PREPARATION

1. Smash avocado in a small bowl with lime juice and salt.
2. Mix in eggs.
3. Divide the mixture between tortillas and top each with 1/2 cup spinach and 1 tablespoon each cheese and salsa.

Calories: 121
Fat: 1g
Carbs: 12g
Protein: 7g

FRUIT & YOGURT SMOOTHIE

INGREDIENTS

- 3/4 cup nonfat plain yogurt
- 1/2 cup 100% pure fruit juice
- 1 1/2 cups (6 1/2 ounces) frozen fruit, such as blueberries, raspberries, pineapple or peaches

PREPARATION

1. Blend yogurt and juice until completely smooth. Fruit should be added through the lid's hole while the engine is running, and it should be pureed until smooth.

Calories: 99
Fat: 2g
Carbs: 15g
Protein: 8g

BREAKFAST SALAD WITH EGG & SALSA VERDE VINAIGRETTE

INGREDIENTS

- 3 tablespoons salsa verde, such as Frontera brand
- 1 tablespoon plus 1 tsp. extra-virgin olive oil, divided
- 2 tablespoons chopped cilantro, plus more for garnish
- 2 cups mesclun or other salad greens
- 8 blue corn tortilla chips, broken into large pieces
- ½ cup canned red kidney beans, rinsed
- ¼ avocado, sliced
- 1 large egg

PREPARATION

1. In a small bowl, combine cilantro, salsa, and 1 tablespoon of oil. Place half of the mixture in a shallow dinner bowl with the mesclun (or other greens).
2. Top the salad with a layer of chips, beans, and avocado.
3. Heat the remaining 1 tsp. oil in a small nonstick skillet over medium-high heat. Add egg and cook for about two minutes, or until the white is fully cooked but the yolk is still a little runny.
4. Serve the salad with the egg. Add more cilantro, if desired, and drizzle with the leftover salsa vinaigrette.

Calories: 167
Fat: 9g
Carbs: 22g
Protein: 11g

MANGO-GINGER SMOOTHIE

INGREDIENTS

- ½ cup cooked red lentils (see Tips), cooled
- 1 cup frozen mango chunks
- ¾ cup carrot juice
- 1 teaspoon chopped fresh ginger
- 1 teaspoon honey
- Pinch of ground cardamom, plus more for garnish
- 3 ice cubes

PREPARATION

1. In a blender, combine the lentils, mango, carrot juice, ginger, honey, cardamom, and ice cubes.
2. Blend on high for 2 to 3 minutes, or until very smooth. If desired, add extra cardamom as a garnish.

Calories: 85
Fat: 1g
Carbs: 10g
Protein: 3g

WHITE BEAN & AVOCADO TOAST

INGREDIENTS

- 1 slice whole-wheat bread, toasted
- ¼ avocado, mashed
- ½ cup canned white beans, rinsed and drained
- Kosher salt to taste
- Ground pepper to taste
- 1 pinch Crushed red pepper

PREPARATION

1. White beans and mashed avocado go well on toast.
2. Add a sprinkle of salt, pepper, and crushed red pepper to taste.

Calories: 120
Fat: 9g
Carbs: 21g
Protein: 9g

VEGAN SMOOTHIE BOWL

1 SERVING

DIFFICULT

COST

INGREDIENTS

- 1 large banana
- 1 cup frozen mixed berries
- ½ cup unsweetened soymilk or other unsweetened non-dairy milk
- ¼ cup pineapple chunks
- ½ kiwi, sliced
- 1 tablespoon sliced almonds, toasted if desired
- 1 tablespoon unsweetened coconut flakes, toasted if desired
- 1 teaspoon chia seeds

PREPARATION

1. In a blender, combine the banana, berries, and soymilk (or almond milk). Until smooth, blend.
2. Then, add the pineapple, kiwi, almonds, coconut, and chia seeds to the smoothie's bowl as garnish.

Calories: 89
Fat: 5g
Carbs: 14g
Protein: 9g

PEANUT BUTTER-BANANA CINNAMON TOAST

INGREDIENTS

- 1 slice whole-wheat bread, toasted
- 1 tablespoon peanut butter
- 1 small banana, sliced
- Cinnamon to taste

PREPARATION

1. Spread toast with peanut butter and top with banana slices.
2. Sprinkle with cinnamon to taste.

Calories: 266
Fat: 9g
Carbs: 38g
Protein: 8g

CANTALOUPE SMOOTHIE

INGREDIENTS

- 1 banana
- 2 cups chopped ripe cantaloupe
- 1/2 cup nonfat or low-fat plain yogurt
- 2 tablespoons nonfat dry milk
- 1 ½ tablespoons frozen orange juice concentrate
- ½ teaspoon vanilla extract

PREPARATION

1. Place unpeeled banana in the freezer overnight (or for up to 3 months).
2. Remove the banana from the freezer and let it sit until the skin begins to soften, about 2 minutes.
3. Remove the skin with a paring knife. (Don't worry if a little fiber remains.)
4. Cut the banana into chunks.
5. Add to a blender or food processor along with cantaloupe, yogurt, dry milk, orange juice and vanilla.
6. Blend until smooth.

Calories: 364
Fat: 3g
Carbs: 75g
Protein: 14g

SPINACH-AVOCADO SMOOTHIE

INGREDIENTS

- 1 cup nonfat plain yogurt
- 1 cup fresh spinach
- 1 frozen banana
- ¼ avocado
- 2 tablespoons water
- 1 teaspoon honey

PREPARATION

1. Combine yogurt, spinach, banana, avocado, water and honey in a blender.
2. Puree until smooth.

Calories: 257
Fat: 8g
Carbs: 28g
Protein: 16g

Meal

CHIPOTLE-LIME CAULIFLOWER TACO BOWLS

INGREDIENTS

- ¼ cup lime juice (from about 2 limes)
- 1-2 tablespoons chopped chipotles in adobo sauce (see Tip)
- 1 tablespoon honey
- 2 cloves garlic
- ½ teaspoon salt
- 1 small head cauliflower, cut into bite-size pieces
- 1 small red onion, halved and thinly sliced
- 2 cups cooked quinoa, cooled (see Associated Recipes)
- 1 cup no-salt-added canned black beans, rinsed
- ½ cup crumbled queso fresco
- 1 cup shredded red cabbage
- 1 medium avocado
- 1 lime, cut into 4 wedges (Optional)

PREPARATION

1. Set the oven to 450 degrees. Wrap foil around a sizable baking sheet with a rim.
2. Blend lime juice, honey, garlic, salt, and chipotles to taste. till largely seamless, process. In a sizable bowl, add the sauce and swirl to coat the cauliflower. To the prepared baking sheet, transfer. Toss onion on top of the cauliflower. Roast for 18 to 20 minutes, tossing once, until the cauliflower is fork-tender and browned in places. Remove from the oven and let cool.
3. Distribute the quinoa (one-half cup each) among 4 single-serving covered containers. Add two tablespoons of cheese, 1/4 cup of the black beans, and 1/4 of the cauliflower mixture to each. For up to 4 days, seal the containers and keep them chilled.
4. To reheat 1 container, vent the lid and microwave on High until steaming, 2 1/2 to 3 minutes. Top with 1/4 cup cabbage and 1/4 avocado (sliced). Serve with a lime wedge, if desired.

Calories: 76
Fat: 2g
Carbs: 17g
Protein: 6g

VEGGIE & HUMMUS SANDWICH

INGREDIENTS

- 2 slices whole-grain bread
- 3 tablespoons hummus
- ¼ avocado, mashed
- ½ cup mixed salad greens
- ¼ medium red bell pepper, sliced
- ¼ cup sliced cucumber
- ¼ cup shredded carrot

PREPARATION

1. Spread hummus on one slice of bread and avocado on the other.
2. Add greens, bell pepper, cucumber, and carrot to the sandwich.
3. Cut in half, then present.

Calories: 125
Fat: 7g
Carbs: 20g
Protein: 13g

SPINACH & STRAWBERRY MEAL-PREP SALAD

INGREDIENTS

- 1 pound boneless, skinless chicken thighs
- ½ teaspoon kosher salt
- ½ teaspoon dried thyme
- ½ teaspoon ground pepper
- 8 cups baby spinach
- 2 cups sliced strawberries
- ¼ cup feta cheese (Optional)
- ¼ cup chopped toasted walnuts
- 6 tablespoons Balsamic Vinaigrette

PREPARATION

1. Set oven to 400 degrees Fahrenheit. Cover a baking sheet with foil or parchment paper.
2. On the prepared baking sheet, put the chicken. Add pepper, thyme, and salt liberally all over. Cook for 15 to 17 minutes, tossing the chicken once, or until the internal temperature of the chicken reaches 165°F. Slice into bite-sized pieces after setting aside to cool.
3. Divide the spinach into four 2-cup single-serving covered containers. Each dish should have one-fourth of the chicken slices, half a cup of strawberry slices, one spoonful of feta (if using), and one tablespoon of walnuts on top.
4. For up to 4 days, place the sealed salad containers in the refrigerator.
5. For up to 5 days, place 1 1/2 tablespoons of vinaigrette in each of 4 little closed containers.
6. Dress the salads with the vinaigrette just before serving.

Calories: 66
Fat: 3g
Carbs: 14g
Protein: 6g

SMOKED SALMON SALAD NICOISE

INGREDIENTS

- ½ small cucumber, halved, seeded and thinly sliced
- 12 small cherry or grape tomatoes, halved
- 4 ounces smoked salmon, cut into 2-inch pieces
- 8 ounces small red potatoes, scrubbed and halved
- 6 ounces green beans, preferably thin haricots verts, trimmed and halved
- 2 tablespoons reduced-fat mayonnaise
- 1 tablespoon white-wine vinegar
- 1 teaspoon lemon juice
- 1 teaspoon Worcestershire sauce
- 1 teaspoon Dijon mustard
- ½ teaspoon dried dill
- ¼ teaspoon freshly ground pepper
- 6 cups mixed salad greens

PREPARATION

1. Place a large bowl of ice water next to the stove. Bring 1 inch of water to a boil in a large saucepan.
2. Place potatoes in a steamer basket over the boiling water, cover and steam until tender when pierced with a fork, 10 to 15 minutes. Transfer the potatoes with a slotted spoon to the ice water.
3. Add green beans to the steamer, cover and steam until tender-crisp, 4 to 5 minutes. Transfer the green beans with a slotted spoon to the ice water.
4. Transfer the potatoes and beans to a towel-lined baking sheet to drain.
5. Meanwhile, whisk mayonnaise, vinegar, lemon juice, Worcestershire sauce, mustard, dill and pepper in a large bowl. Add the potatoes and green beans, salad greens, cucumber and tomatoes; toss gently to coat.
6. Divide the salad and smoked salmon between 2 plates.

Calories: 271
Fat: 11g
Carbs: 19g
Protein: 17g

SWEET POTATO, KALE & CHICKEN SALAD WITH PEANUT DRESSING

4 SERVINGS

DIFFICULT

COST

INGREDIENTS

- 1 pound sweet potatoes (about 2 medium), scrubbed and cut into 1-inch cubes
- 1 ½ teaspoons extra-virgin olive oil
- ¼ teaspoon kosher salt
- ⅛ teaspoon ground pepper
- 1/2 cup Peanut Dressing (see Associated Recipes)
- 6 cups chopped curly kale
- 2 cups shredded cooked chicken breast (see Tip)
- ¼ cup chopped unsalted peanuts

PREPARATION

1. Set oven to 425 degrees Fahrenheit. A rimmed baking sheet should be lined with foil and lightly sprayed with cooking spray. Place aside. Sweet potatoes should be mixed with oil, salt, and pepper in a big dish.
2. Place the sweet potatoes on the baking sheet that has been prepared in a single layer. Roast for about 20 minutes, tossing once, until fork-tender and lightly browned and crispy on the exterior. Before putting together bowls, set aside to chill.
3. Put two tablespoons of peanut dressing into each of four tiny containers with lids, and then store in the fridge for up to four days.
4. Divide the kale (approximately 1 1/2 cups total) among the 4 single-serving containers. Top each with 1/4 of the sweet potatoes that have been cooked and 1/2 cup of the chicken. For up to 4 days, seal the containers and keep them chilled.
5. Just before serving, drizzle each salad with 1 portion of peanut dressing and toss well to coat. Top with 1 tablespoon chopped peanuts

Calories: 293
Fat: 9g
Carbs: 32g
Protein: 12g

MEAL-PREP VEGAN LETTUCE WRAPS

4 SERVINGS

DIFFICULT

COST

INGREDIENTS

- 2 heads butter or Bibb lettuce, leaves separated
- 1 1/2 cups cooked quinoa, cooled to room temperature (see Associated Recipes)
- 4 cups Bean Salad with Lemon-Cumin Dressing (see Associated Recipes)
- ⅓ cup chopped fresh mint (reserved from bean salad recipe)

PREPARATION

1. To prepare 1 serving of lettuce wraps: Place 3 lettuce leaves in a single-serving lidded container. Top each leaf with 2 tablespoons quinoa and 1/3 cup bean salad.
2. Sprinkle each with 1 1/2 teaspoons mint. Refrigerate for up to 1 day.

Calories: 425
Fat: 20g
Carbs: 50g
Protein: 14g

MASON JAR POWER SALAD WITH CHICKPEAS & TUNA

4 SERVINGS

DIFFICULT

COST

INGREDIENTS

- 3 cups bite-sized pieces chopped kale
- 2 tablespoons honey-mustard vinaigrette (see associated recipe)
- 1 2.5-ounce pouch tuna in water
- ½ cup rinsed canned chickpeas
- 1 carrot, peeled and shredded

PREPARATION

1. Toss kale and dressing in a bowl, then tranfer to a 1-quart mason jar.
2. Top with tuna, chickpeas and carrot. Screw lid onto the jar and refrigerate for up to 2 days.
3. To serve, empty the jar contents into a bowl and toss to combine the salad ingredients with the dressed kale.

Calories: 430
Fat: 23g
Carbs: 30g
Protein: 26g

WINTER KALE & QUINOA SALAD WITH AVOCADO

INGREDIENTS

- 1 small sweet potato, peeled and cut into 1/2-inch pieces (1 1/2 cups)
- 2 ½ teaspoons olive oil, divided
- ½ avocado
- 1 tablespoon lime juice
- 1 clove garlic, peeled
- ½ teaspoon ground cumin
- ⅛ teaspoon salt
- ⅛ teaspoon ground pepper
- 1-2 tablespoons water
- 1 cup cooked quinoa (see Associated Recipes)
- ¾ cup no-salt-added canned black beans, rinsed
- 1 ½ cups chopped baby kale
- 2 tablespoons pepitas (see Tip)
- 1 scallion, chopped

PREPARATION

1. Set oven to 400 degrees Fahrenheit.
2. On a sizable rimmed baking sheet, toss sweet potatoes with 1 teaspoon oil. Roast for about 25 minutes, stirring once halfway through, until fork-tender.
3. In the meantime, blend or process the remaining 1 1/2 teaspoons of oil, avocado, lime juice, garlic, cumin, salt, and pepper along with 1 tablespoon of water until smooth. If necessary, add 1 Tbsp. water to achieve the appropriate consistency.
4. In a medium bowl, mix the kale, black beans, sweet potatoes, and quinoa. Add the avocado dressing and toss to evenly coat. Add pepitas and scallion on top.

Calories: 189
Fat: 10g
Carbs: 24g
Protein: 15g

VEGAN SUPERFOOD GRAIN BOWLS

4 SERVINGS

DIFFICULT

COST

INGREDIENTS

- 1 (8 ounce) pouch microwavable quinoa
- ½ cup hummus
- 2 tablespoons lemon juice
- 1 (5 ounce) package baby kale
- 1 (8 ounce) package refrigerated cooked whole baby beets, sliced (or 2 cups from salad bar)
- 1 cup frozen shelled edamame, thawed
- 1 medium avocado, sliced
- ¼ cup unsalted toasted sunflower seeds

Calories: 139
Fat: 4g
Carbs: 24g
Protein: 5g

PREPARATION

1. Prepare quinoa according to package directions; set aside to cool.
2. Combine hummus and lemon juice in a small bowl. Thin with water to desired dressing consistency. Divide the dressing among 4 small condiment containers with lids and refrigerate.
3. Divide baby kale among 4 single-serving containers with lids. Top each with 1/2 cup of the quinoa, 1/2 cup beets, 1/4 cup edamame and 1 tablespoon sunflower seeds.
4. When ready to eat, top with 1/4 avocado and the hummus dressing.

SLOW-COOKER CHICKEN & CHICKPEA SOUP

INGREDIENTS

- 1 ½ cups dried chickpeas, soaked overnight
- 4 cups water
- 1 large yellow onion, finely chopped
- 1 (15 ounce) can no-salt-added diced tomatoes, preferably fire-roasted
- 2 tablespoons tomato paste
- 4 cloves garlic, finely chopped
- 1 bay leaf
- 4 teaspoons ground cumin
- 4 teaspoons paprika
- ¼ teaspoon cayenne pepper
- ¼ teaspoon ground pepper
- 2 pounds bone-in chicken thighs, skin removed, trimmed
- 1 (14 ounce) can artichoke hearts, drained and quartered
- ¼ cup halved pitted oil-cured olives
- ½ teaspoon salt
- ¼ cup chopped fresh parsley or cilantro

PREPARATION

1. Chickpeas should be drained and added to a 6-quart or larger slow cooker. Stir together the water, onion, tomatoes, tomato juice, tomato paste, bay leaf, cumin, paprika, cayenne, and pepper. Add, Cook, and cover for 8 hours on low or 4 hours on high.
2. Place the chicken on a spotless cutting board, then allow it to cool slightly. Remove the bay leaf. add the artichokes, olives, and salt in the slow cooker.
3. Discard the chicken's bones as you shred it. Add the chicken to the soup and stir. Serve garnished with cilantro or parsley.

Calories: 77
Fats: 4g
Crabs: 17g
Protein: 6g

ROASTED ROOT VEGETABLES WITH GOAT CHEESE POLENTA

2 SERVINGS
DIFFICULT
COST

INGREDIENTS

- Polenta:
- 2 cups low-sodium vegetable or chicken broth
- ½ cup polenta fine cornmeal or corn grits
- ¼ cup goat cheese
- 1 tablespoon extra-virgin olive oil or butter
- ¼ teaspoon kosher salt
- ¼ teaspoon ground pepper
- Vegetables:
- 1 tablespoon extra-virgin olive oil or butter
- 1 clove garlic, smashed
- 2 cups roasted root vegetables (see associated recipes)
- 1 tablespoon torn fresh sage
- 2 teaspoons prepared pesto
- Fresh parsley for garnish

PREPARATION

1. To prepare polenta: Bring broth to a boil in a medium saucepan. Reduce heat to low and gradually add polenta (or cornmeal or grits), whisking vigorously to avoid clumping. Cover and cook for 10 minutes. Stir, cover and continue cooking until thickened and creamy, about 10 minutes more.
2. Stir in goat cheese, oil (or butter), salt and pepper.
3. To prepare vegetables: Heat oil (or butter) in a medium skillet over medium heat.
4. Add garlic and cook, stirring, until fragrant, about 1 minute. Add roasted vegetables and cook, stirring often, until heated through, 2 to 4 minutes.
5. Stir in sage and cook until fragrant, about 1 minute more.
6. Serve the vegetables over the polenta, topped with pesto. Garnish with parsley, if desired.

Calories: 162
Fat: 8g
Carbs: 21g
Protein: 9g

EGGPLANT PARMESAN

6 SERVINGS
DIFFICULT
COST

INGREDIENTS

- Canola or olive oil cooking spray
- 2 large eggs
- 2 tablespoons water
- 1 cup panko breadcrumbs
- ¾ cup grated Parmesan cheese, divided
- 1 teaspoon Italian seasoning
- 2 medium eggplants (about 2 pounds total), cut crosswise into ¼-inch-thick slices
- ½ teaspoon salt
- ½ teaspoon ground pepper
- 1 (24 ounce) jar no-salt-added tomato sauce
- ¼ cup fresh basil leaves, torn, plus more for serving
- 2 cloves garlic, grated
- ½ teaspoon crushed red pepper
- 1 cup shredded part-skim mozzarella cheese, divided

Calories: 241
Fat: 9g
Carbs: 28g
Protein: 14g

PREPARATION

1. Position racks in middle and lower thirds of oven; preheat to 400°F. Coat 2 baking sheets and a 9-by-13-inch baking dish with cooking spray.
2. Whisk eggs and water in a shallow bowl. Mix breadcrumbs, 1/4 cup Parmesan and Italian seasoning in another shallow dish. Dip eggplant in the egg mixture, then coat with the breadcrumb mixture, gently pressing to adhere.
3. Arrange the eggplant in a single layer on the prepared baking sheets. Generously spray both sides of the eggplant with cooking spray.
4. Bake, flipping the eggplant and switching the pans between racks halfway, until the eggplant is tender and lightly browned, about 30 minutes. Season with salt and pepper.
5. Meanwhile, mix tomato sauce, basil, garlic and crushed red pepper in a medium bowl.
6. Spread about 1/2 cup of the sauce in the prepared baking dish. Arrange half the eggplant slices over the sauce.
7. Spoon 1 cup sauce over the eggplant and sprinkle with 1/4 cup Parmesan and 1/2 cup mozzarella. Top with the remaining eggplant, sauce and cheese.
8. Bake until the sauce is bubbling and the top is golden, 20 to 30 minutes.
9. Let cool for 5 minutes. Sprinkle with more basil before serving, if desired.

CHICKEN-QUINOA BOWL WITH OLIVES & CUCUMBER

4 SERVINGS

DIFFICULT

COST

INGREDIENTS

- 1 pound boneless, skinless chicken breasts, trimmed
- ¼ teaspoon salt
- ¼ teaspoon ground pepper
- 1 7-ounce jar roasted red peppers, rinsed
- ¼ cup slivered almonds
- 4 tablespoons extra-virgin olive oil, divided
- 1 small clove garlic, crushed
- 1 teaspoon paprika
- ½ teaspoon ground cumin
- ¼ teaspoon crushed red pepper (Optional)
- 2 cups cooked quinoa
- ¼ cup pitted Kalamata olives, chopped
- ¼ cup finely chopped red onion
- 1 cup diced cucumber
- ¼ cup crumbled feta cheese
- 2 tablespoons finely chopped fresh parsley

PREPARATION

1. Place a rack in the upper third of the oven and turn the broiler to high. Use foil to cover a baking sheet with a rim.
2. Place the chicken on the prepared baking sheet, seasoning with salt and pepper.
3. For 14 to 18 minutes, broil, stirring once, until an instant-read thermometer inserted in the thickest section registers 165 degrees F. Slice or shred the chicken after moving it to a clean cutting board.
4. In the meantime, combine the peppers, almonds, 2 tablespoons of oil, the garlic, paprika, cumin, and any crushed red pepper you're using in a small food processor. until largely smooth, puree.
5. In a medium bowl, mix the quinoa, olives, red onion, and the last 2 tablespoons of oil.
6. Divide the quinoa mixture among four bowls to serve, then top each with equal quantities of cucumber, chicken, and the red pepper sauce. Sprinkle with feta and parsley.

Calories: 291
Fat: 7g
Carbs: 21g
Protein: 14g

WALNUT-ROSEMARY CRUSTED SALMON

INGREDIENTS

- 2 teaspoons Dijon mustard
- 1 clove garlic, minced
- ¼ teaspoon lemon zest
- 1 teaspoon lemon juice
- 1 teaspoon chopped fresh rosemary
- ½ teaspoon honey
- ½ teaspoon kosher salt
- ¼ teaspoon crushed red pepper
- 3 tablespoons panko breadcrumbs
- 3 tablespoons finely chopped walnuts
- 1 teaspoon extra-virgin olive oil
- 1 (1 pound) skinless salmon fillet, fresh or frozen
- Olive oil cooking spray
- Chopped fresh parsley and lemon wedges for garnish

PREPARATION

1. Set oven to 425 degrees Fahrenheit. Use parchment paper to line a big baking sheet with a rim.
2. In a small bowl, mix the mustard, garlic, lemon zest, lemon juice, rosemary, honey, salt, and red pepper flakes. In a different small bowl, mix the panko, walnuts, and oil.
3. On the prepared baking sheet, put the fish. After applying the mustard mixture to the fish, sprinkle the panko mixture over it and press firmly to help it stick. Apply cooking spray sparingly.
4. Depending on thickness, bake the fish for 8 to 12 minutes, or until it flakes easily with a fork.
5. If preferred, serve with lemon wedges and garnish with parsley.

Calories: 222
Fat: 12g
Carbs: 21g
Protein: 14g

HASSELBACK EGGPLANT PARMESAN

INGREDIENTS

- 1 cup prepared low-sodium marinara sauce
- 4 small eggplants (about 6 inches long; 1 3/4 pounds total)
- 2 tablespoons extra-virgin olive oil plus 2 teaspoons, divided
- 4 ounces fresh mozzarella, thinly sliced into 12 pieces
- ¼ cup prepared pesto
- ½ cup whole-wheat panko breadcrumbs
- 2 tablespoons grated Parmesan cheese
- 1 tablespoon chopped fresh basil

PREPARATION

1. Set oven to 375 degrees Fahrenheit.
2. In a 9 by 13-inch baking dish that may be used for broiling, spread sauce. Slice each eggplant crosswise every 1/4 inch, almost to the bottom but not all the way through. Transfer the eggplants with care to the baking pan. To make the cuts more visible, gently fan them.
3. Sprinkle the eggplants with 2 tablespoons of oil. Alternately place mozzarella and pesto inside the cuts; some cuts might not be filled. Wrap with foil.
4. Bake the eggplants for 45 to 55 minutes, or until very soft.
5. In a separate dish, mix the remaining 2 teaspoons oil, panko, and Parmesan. Take off the foil and sprinkle the breadcrumb mixture over the eggplants.
6. Increase the oven temperature to broil. The topping should be golden brown after 2 to 4 minutes of broiling the eggplants on the center rack. Add basil on top. With the sauce, serve.

Calories: 349
Fat: 11g
Carbs: 24g
Protein: 11g

CHICKEN & VEGETABLE PENNE WITH PARSLEY-WALNUT PESTO

4 SERVINGS

DIFFICULT

COST

INGREDIENTS

- ¾ cup chopped walnuts
- 1 cup lightly packed parsley leaves
- 2 cloves garlic, crushed and peeled
- ½ teaspoon plus 1/8 teaspoon salt
- ⅛ teaspoon ground pepper
- 2 tablespoons olive oil
- ⅓ cup grated Parmesan cheese
- 1 ½ cups shredded or sliced cooked skinless chicken breast (8 oz.)
- 6 ounces whole-wheat penne or fusilli pasta (1 3/4 cups)
- 8 ounces green beans, trimmed and halved crosswise (2 cups)
- 2 cups cauliflower florets (8 oz.)

Calories: 414
Fat: 7g
Carbs: 23g
Protein: 18g

PREPARATION

1. Bring water in a big pot to a boil.
2. In a small bowl, add the walnuts. Microwave on High for 2 to 2 1/2 minutes, or until fragrant and lightly toasted. (Alternatively, toast the walnuts for 2 to 3 minutes, stirring regularly, in a small, dry skillet over medium-low heat.) Place on a plate and allow to cool. Set aside 1/4 cup for the topping.
3. In a food processor, mix the remaining 1/2 cup of walnuts, parsley, garlic, salt, and pepper. Process the nuts until they are powdered. Oil should be added gradually through the feed tube while the motor is operating. Then pulse to incorporate the Parmesan. Put the pesto in a big bowl by scraping it. Add chicken.
4. During this time, cook the pasta for 4 minutes in the boiling water. Add the cauliflower and green beans; cover the pan and cook for an additional 5 to 7 minutes, or until the veggies are soft and the pasta is almost done.
5. Scoop off 3/4 cup of the cooking liquid before draining, then swirl it into the pesto-chicken combination to slightly warm it.
6. Add the pasta and vegetables after draining them to the chicken and pesto mixture. Toss to evenly coat.
7. Top each meal with one tablespoon of the saved walnuts after dividing among the four spaghetti bowls.

SHEET-PAN CHICKEN WITH ROASTED SPRING VEGETABLES & LEMON

4 SERVINGS

DIFFICULT

COST

INGREDIENTS

- Lemon Vinaigrette
- 1 lemon
- 1 tablespoon olive oil
- 1 tablespoon crumbled feta cheese
- ½ teaspoon honey
- Greek Chicken with Roasted Spring Vegetables
- 2 (8 ounce) skinless, boneless chicken breast halves, cut in half lengthwise
- ¼ cup light mayonnaise
- 6 cloves garlic, minced
- ½ cup panko bread crumbs
- 3 tablespoons grated Parmesan cheese
- ½ teaspoon kosher salt
- ½ teaspoon black pepper
- Nonstick olive oil cooking spray
- 2 cups 1-inch pieces asparagus
- 1 ½ cups sliced fresh cremini mushrooms
- 1 ½ cups halved grape tomatoes
- 1 tablespoon olive oil
- Snipped fresh dill

PREPARATION

1. Prepare vinaigrette: Remove 1/2 teaspoon zest and squeeze 1 tablespoon juice from lemon. In a small bowl whisk together lemon zest and juice and the remaining ingredients. Set aside.
2. Prepare chicken and vegetables:
3. Place a 15x10-inch baking pan in oven. Preheat oven to 475 degrees F.
4. Meanwhile, using the flat side of a meat mallet, flatten chicken between two pieces of plastic wrap until 1/2 inch thick.
5. Place chicken in a medium bowl. Add mayonnaise and 2 of the garlic cloves; stir to coat. In a shallow dish stir together bread crumbs, cheese, 1/4 teaspoon of the salt, and 1/4 teaspoon of the pepper. Dip chicken into crumb mixture, turning to coat. Lightly coat tops of chicken with cooking spray.
6. In a large bowl combine asparagus, mushrooms, tomatoes, oil and the remaining 4 cloves garlic and 1/4 teaspoon salt and pepper.
7. Carefully place chicken in one end of hot pan and place asparagus mixture in other end of pan. Roast 18 to 20 minutes or until chicken is done (165 degrees F) and vegetables are tender.
8. Drizzle chicken and vegetables with vinaigrette and sprinkle with dill.

CHICKEN CAESAR PASTA SALAD

INGREDIENTS

- ½ cup low-fat buttermilk
- ¼ cup low-fat plain Greek yogurt
- 3 tablespoons extra-virgin olive oil
- 2 tablespoons fresh lemon juice
- 2 teaspoons Dijon mustard
- 1 ½ teaspoons anchovy paste
- 1 large garlic clove
- ¾ cup finely grated Parmesan cheese, divided
- ½ teaspoon salt, divided
- ½ teaspoon ground pepper, divided
- 8 ounces whole-wheat penne
- 3 cups shredded cooked chicken breast
- 1 pint cherry tomatoes, halved
- 5 cups chopped romaine lettuce

PREPARATION

1. Blend the buttermilk, yogurt, oil, lemon juice, mustard, anchovy paste, garlic, 1/2 cup Parmesan, 1/4 teaspoon salt, and 1/4 teaspoon pepper in a high-speed blender for about a minute, or until creamy. Place aside.
2. Without adding salt, prepare pasta as directed on the package. Reserving 1 cup of cooking water, drain.
3. In a sizable bowl, combine the pasta, chicken, tomatoes, 1/4 cup of the cooking water that was set aside, and the final 1/4 teaspoons of salt and pepper.
4. Add the buttermilk dressing and stir until well mixed. If more cooking water is required to achieve a creamy consistency, stir it in. For at least 30 minutes or up to two days, cover and chill.
5. Add lettuce and the remaining 1/4 cup Parmesan right before serving.

Calories: 383
Fat: 10g
Carbs: 24g
Protein: 13g

4 SERVINGS

DIFFICULT

COST

DIJON SALMON WITH GREEN BEAN PILAF

INGREDIENTS

- 1 ¼ pounds wild salmon (see Tip), skinned and cut into 4 portions
- 3 tablespoons extra-virgin olive oil, divided
- 1 tablespoon minced garlic
- ¾ teaspoon salt
- 2 tablespoons mayonnaise
- 2 teaspoons whole-grain mustard
- ½ teaspoon ground pepper, divided
- 12 ounces pretrimmed haricots verts or thin green beans, cut into thirds
- 1 small lemon, zested and cut into 4 wedges
- 2 tablespoons pine nuts
- 1 8-ounce package precooked brown rice
- 2 tablespoons water
- Chopped fresh parsley for garnish

PREPARATION

1. Preheat oven to 425 degrees F. Line a rimmed baking sheet with foil or parchment paper.
2. Brush salmon with 1 tablespoon oil and place on the prepared baking sheet. Mash garlic and salt into a paste with the side of a chef's knife or a fork.
3. Combine a scant 1 teaspoon of the garlic paste in a small bowl with mayonnaise, mustard and 1/4 teaspoon pepper. Spread the mixture on top of the fish.
4. Roast the salmon until it flakes easily with a fork in the thickest part, 6 to 8 minutes per inch of thickness.
5. Meanwhile, heat the remaining 2 tablespoons oil in a large skillet over medium-high heat. Add green beans, lemon zest, pine nuts, the remaining garlic paste and 1/4 teaspoon pepper; cook, stirring, until the beans are just tender, 2 to 4 minutes. Reduce heat to medium. Add rice and water and cook, stirring, until hot, 2 to 3 minutes more.
6. Sprinkle the salmon with parsley, if desired, and serve with the green bean pilaf and lemon wedges.

Calories: 442
Fat: 25g
Carbs: 12g
Protein: 32g

SLOW-COOKER VEGETARIAN BOLOGNESE

INGREDIENTS

- 1 (28 ounce) can diced tomatoes, preferably San Marzano
- ½ cup dry white wine
- ½ cup low-sodium vegetable broth or water
- 1 cup chopped onion
- ½ cup chopped celery
- ½ cup chopped carrot
- 3 tablespoons extra-virgin olive oil
- 2 tablespoons minced garlic
- 1 teaspoon Italian seasoning
- ½ teaspoon salt
- ¼ teaspoon ground pepper
- 2 (15 ounce) cans no-salt-added cannellini beans or small white beans, rinsed
- ¼ cup heavy cream
- 1 pound whole-wheat pasta
- ½ cup grated Parmesan cheese
- ¼ cup chopped fresh basil

PREPARATION

1. In a 5- to 6-quart slow cooker, combine the tomatoes, wine, broth (or water), onion, celery, carrot, oil, garlic, Italian seasoning, salt, and pepper.
2. Cook for 4 hours on high or 8 hours on low. At the end of the cooking process, stir in the beans and cream. Stay warm.
3. In the meantime, heat up a sizable pot of water to a boil.
4. Drain spaghetti after cooking it according the directions on the package. 8 bowls should get the pasta. Add basil, Parmesan, and sauce as a garnish.

Calories: 434
Fat: 13g
Carbs: 34g
Protein: 11g

CREAMY LEMON PASTA WITH SHRIMP

4 SERVINGS

DIFFICULT

COST

INGREDIENTS

- 8 ounces whole-wheat fettuccine
- 1 tablespoon extra-virgin olive oil
- 12 ounces peeled and deveined raw shrimp (21-25 count)
- 2 tablespoons unsalted butter
- 1 tablespoon finely chopped garlic
- ¼ teaspoon crushed red pepper
- 4 cups loosely packed arugula
- ¼ cup whole-milk plain yogurt
- 1 teaspoon lemon zest
- 2 tablespoons lemon juice
- ¼ teaspoon salt
- ⅓ cup grated Parmesan cheese, plus more for garnish
- ¼ cup thinly sliced fresh basil

Calories: 403
Fat: 14g
Carbs: 36g
Protein: 18g

PREPARATION

1. 7 cups of water should come to a boil. Stir the fettuccine to separate the noodles before adding. Cook for 7 to 9 minutes, or until the meat is barely tender. After draining, save 1/2 cup of the cooking liquid.
2. Over medium-high heat, warm oil in a sizable nonstick skillet. Add the shrimp and cook, stirring periodically, for 2 to 3 minutes, or until pink and curled. Put the shrimp in a basin.
3. Reduce heat to medium, then add butter to the pan. Stir often while cooking the garlic and crushed red pepper for approximately a minute, or until the garlic is aromatic.
4. Arugula should be added and cooked for about a minute while stirring. Low-heat setting. When the pasta is thoroughly coated and creamy, add the remaining 1/4 cup of cooking water, the yogurt, the lemon zest, and the fettuccine.
5. Add the salt, lemon juice, and shrimp while tossing the fettuccine to coat. Take the dish off the heat, then top with Parmesan.
6. If preferred, top the fettuccine with additional Parmesan and basil.

ROASTED SALMON WITH SMOKY CHICKPEAS & GREENS

INGREDIENTS

- 2 tablespoons extra-virgin olive oil, divided
- 1 tablespoon smoked paprika
- ½ teaspoon salt, divided, plus a pinch
- 1 (15 ounce) can no-salt-added chickpeas, rinsed
- ⅓ cup buttermilk
- ¼ cup mayonnaise
- ¼ cup chopped fresh chives and/or dill, plus more for garnish
- ½ teaspoon ground pepper, divided
- ¼ teaspoon garlic powder
- 10 cups chopped kale
- ¼ cup water
- 1 ¼ pounds wild salmon, cut into 4 portions
- ¼ avocado

Calories: 447
Fat: 22g
Carbs: 23g
Protein: 37g

PREPARATION

1. Position racks in upper third and middle of oven; preheat to 425 degrees F.
2. Combine 1 tablespoon oil, paprika and 1/4 teaspoon salt in a medium bowl. Very thoroughly pat chickpeas dry, then toss with the paprika mixture. Spread on a rimmed baking sheet.
3. Bake the chickpeas on the upper rack, stirring twice, for 30 minutes.
4. Meanwhile, puree buttermilk, mayonnaise, herbs, 1/4 teaspoon pepper and garlic powder in a blender until smooth. Set aside.
5. Heat the remaining 1 tablespoon oil in a large skillet over medium heat. Add kale and cook, stirring occasionally, for 2 minutes.
6. Add water and continue cooking until the kale is tender, about 5 minutes more. Remove from heat and stir in a pinch of salt.
7. Remove the chickpeas from the oven and push them to one side of the pan. Place salmon on the other side and season with the remaining 1/4 teaspoon each salt and pepper. Bake until the salmon is just cooked through, 5 to 8 minutes.
8. Drizzle the reserved dressing on the salmon, garnish with more herbs and avocado, if desired, and serve with the kale and chickpeas.

SLOW-COOKER VEGETARIAN BOLOGNESE

INGREDIENTS

- 2 cups chopped onions
- 1 cup chopped carrots
- 1 cup chopped celery
- 1 pound cooked Meal-Prep Sheet-Pan Chicken Thighs (see associated recipe), diced
- 4 cups cooked whole-wheat rotini pasta
- 6 cups reduced-sodium chicken broth
- 4 teaspoons dried Italian seasoning
- ¼ teaspoon salt
- 1 (15 ounce) can no-salt-added white beans, rinsed
- 4 cups baby spinach (half of a 5-ounce box)
- 4 tablespoons chopped fresh basil, divided (Optional)
- 2 tablespoons best-quality extra-virgin olive oil
- ½ cup grated Parmigiano-Reggiano cheese

PREPARATION

1. Put celery, carrots, and onions in a sizable plastic bag that can be sealed. Place cooked pasta and cold chicken in a separate bag.
2. Freeze for up to five days after sealing both bags. Before continuing, let the bags defrost overnight in the fridge.
3. Transfer the vegetable mixture to a large slow cooker. Add broth, Italian seasoning, and salt. Cover and cook on Low for 7 1/4 hours.
4. Add the defrosted chicken, pasta, beans, spinach, and any additional 2 tablespoons of basil.
5. Cook for a further 45 minutes. Put the soup in bowls by ladling. Add a few drops of oil to each bowl before adding cheese and, if wanted, the final 2 tablespoons of basil.

Calories: 457
Fat: 14g
Carbs: 32g
Protein: 14g

SALMON COUSCOUS SALAD

INGREDIENTS

- ¼ cup sliced cremini mushrooms
- ¼ cup diced eggplant
- 3 cups baby spinach
- 2 tablespoons white-wine vinaigrette, divided (see Tip)
- ¼ cup cooked Israeli couscous, preferably whole-wheat
- 4 ounces cooked salmon
- ¼ cup sliced dried apricots
- 2 tablespoons crumbled goat cheese (1/2 ounce)

PREPARATION

1. Apply cooking spray to a small skillet and heat it over medium-high heat. Add the mushrooms and eggplant; simmer, stirring occasionally, for 3 to 5 minutes, or until the juices have released. Heat has been removed; set aside.
2. Put spinach on a 9-inch platter and toss with 1 Tbsp plus 1 tsp of vinaigrette.
3. Place the couscous on top of the spinach and toss with the remaining 2 teaspoons of vinaigrette. Afterward, add the salmon.
4. Add goat cheese, dried apricots, and cooked vegetables on top.

Calories: 464
Fat: 22g
Carbs: 35g
Protein: 25g

QUINOA POWER SALAD

2 SERVINGS

DIFFICULT

COST

INGREDIENTS

- 1 medium sweet potato, peeled and cut into 1/2-inch-thick wedges
- ½ red onion, cut into 1/4-inch-thick wedges
- 2 tablespoons extra-virgin olive oil, divided
- ½ teaspoon garlic powder
- ¼ teaspoon salt, divided
- 8 ounces chicken tenders
- 2 tablespoons whole-grain mustard, divided
- 1 tablespoon finely chopped shallot
- 1 tablespoon pure maple syrup
- 1 tablespoon cider vinegar
- 4 cups baby greens, such as spinach, kale and/or arugula, washed and dried
- ½ cup cooked red quinoa, cooled
- 1 tablespoon unsalted sunflower seeds, toasted
- 3 tomatoes

Calories: 266
Fat: 5g
Carbs: 25g
Protein: 11g

PREPARATION

1. Set oven to 425 degrees Fahrenheit. In a larger bowl, combine sweet potato and onion with 1 tablespoon oil, 1/8 teaspoon salt, and garlic powder. Spread out and roast for 15 minutes on a big baking sheet with a rim.
2. In the meantime, add the chicken to the bowl and stir in 1 tablespoon of mustard. Remove the vegetables from the oven after 15 minutes of roasting and toss.
3. To the pan, add the chicken. Return to the oven and roast for an additional 10 minutes or until the chicken is fully cooked and the vegetables are starting to brown. Take out of the oven, then allow to cool.
4. In the meantime, combine the shallot, vinegar, maple syrup, 1 tablespoon of residual oil, 1 tablespoon of mustard, and 1/8 teaspoon of salt in the big bowl.
5. Once the chicken has cooled, shred it and add it to the dressing in a bowl. Add the roasted vegetables, sliced tomatoes, quinoa, and baby greens. Add the sunflower seeds and toss with the dressing.

SLOW-COOKER CHICKEN & ORZO WITH TOMATOES & OLIVES

4 SERVINGS
DIFFICULT
COST

INGREDIENTS

- 1 pound boneless, skinless chicken breasts, trimmed
- 1 cup low-sodium chicken broth
- 2 medium tomatoes, chopped
- 1 medium onion, halved and sliced
- Zest and juice of 1 lemon
- 1 teaspoon herbes de Provence
- ½ teaspoon salt
- ½ teaspoon ground pepper
- ¾ cup whole-wheat orzo
- ⅓ cup quartered black or green olives
- 2 tablespoons chopped fresh parsley

PREPARATION

1. Cut each half of a chicken breast into four pieces. In a 6-quart slow cooker, mix the chicken, broth, tomatoes, onion, lemon zest, lemon juice, herbes de Provence, salt, and pepper.
2. Cook for 1 hour and 30 minutes on high or 3 hours and 30 minutes on low.
3. Add the orzo and olives, cover, and simmer for an additional 30 minutes or until the orzo is cooked. Allow to cool a bit.
4. Parsley should be added just before serving.

Calories: 278
Fat: 5g
Carbs: 30g
Protein: 29g

SALMON & ASPARAGUS WITH LEMON-GARLIC BUTTER SAUCE

INGREDIENTS

- 1 pound center-cut salmon fillet, preferably wild, cut into 4 portions
- 1 pound fresh asparagus, trimmed
- ½ teaspoon salt
- ½ teaspoon ground pepper
- 3 tablespoons butter
- 1 tablespoon extra-virgin olive oil
- ½ tablespoon grated garlic
- 1 teaspoon grated lemon zest
- 1 tablespoon lemon juice

Calories: 270
Fat: 15g
Carbs: 12g
Protein: 20g

PREPARATION

1. Set oven to 375 degrees Fahrenheit. Spray cooking oil on a sizable baking sheet with a rim.
2. Place the asparagus and salmon on opposite sides of the baking sheet that has been prepared. Add salt and pepper to the fish and asparagus.
3. In a small skillet over medium heat, combine the butter, oil, garlic, lemon juice, and zest. Cook until the butter is melted. Over the salmon and asparagus, drizzle the butter mixture.
4. Bake for 12 to 15 minutes, or until the salmon is thoroughly cooked and the asparagus is barely tender.

ONE-POT GARLICKY SHRIMP & SPINACH

INGREDIENTS

- 3 tablespoons extra-virgin olive oil, divided
- 6 medium cloves garlic, sliced, divided
- 1 pound spinach
- ¼ teaspoon salt plus 1/8 teaspoon, divided
- 1 ½ teaspoons lemon zest
- 1 tablespoon lemon juice
- 1 pound shrimp (21-30 count), peeled and deveined
- ¼ teaspoon crushed red pepper
- 1 tablespoon finely chopped fresh parsley

PREPARATION

1. Heat 1 tablespoon oil in a large pot over medium heat. Add half the garlic and cook until beginning to brown, 1 to 2 minutes.
2. Add spinach and 1/4 teaspoon salt and toss to coat. Cook, stirring once or twice, until mostly wilted, 3 to 5 minutes. Remove from heat and stir in lemon juice. Transfer to a bowl and keep warm.
3. Increase heat to medium-high and add the remaining 2 tablespoons oil to the pot. Add the remaining garlic and cook until beginning to brown, 1 to 2 minutes.
4. Add shrimp, crushed red pepper and the remaining 1/8 teaspoon salt; cook, stirring, until the shrimp are just cooked through, 3 to 5 minutes more.
5. Serve the shrimp over the spinach, sprinkled with lemon zest and parsley.

Calories: 226
Fat: 12g
Carbs: 6g
Protein: 26g

FIG & GOAT CHEESE SALAD

INGREDIENTS

- 2 cups mixed salad greens
- 4 dried figs, stemmed and sliced
- 1 ounce fresh goat cheese, crumbled
- 1 ½ tablespoons slivered almonds, preferably toasted
- 2 teaspoons extra-virgin olive oil
- 2 teaspoons balsamic vinegar
- ½ teaspoon honey
- Pinch of salt
- Freshly ground pepper to taste

PREPARATION

1. Combine greens, figs, goat cheese and almonds in a medium bowl. Stir together oil, vinegar, honey, salt and pepper.
2. Just before serving, drizzle the dressing over the salad and toss.

Calories: 140
Fat: 9g
Carbs: 32g
Protein: 10g

CHICKEN PESTO PASTA WITH ASPARAGUS

INGREDIENTS

- 8 ounces whole-wheat penne
- 1 pound fresh asparagus, trimmed and cut into 2-inch pieces
- 3 cups shredded cooked chicken breast
- 1 (7 ounce) container refrigerated basil pesto
- 1 teaspoon salt
- ¼ teaspoon ground pepper
- 1 ounce Parmesan cheese, grated (about 1/4 cup)
- Small fresh basil leaves for garnish

PREPARATION

1. According to the directions on the package, cook the pasta in a big saucepan. Asparagus should be added to the pot during the last two minutes of cooking. Reserving 1/2 cup of cooking water, drain.
2. Add the chicken, pesto, salt, and pepper to the spaghetti mixture before adding it back to the saucepan.
3. To get the appropriate consistency, stir in the reserved cooking water, 1 tablespoon at a time.
4. Transfer the mixture to a serving dish, top with Parmesan, and, if preferred, add basil. Serve right away.

Calories: 422
Fat: 9g
Carbs: 25g
Protein: 14g

EASY SALMON CAKES

4 SERVINGS

DIFFICULT

COST

INGREDIENTS

- 3 teaspoons extra-virgin olive oil, divided
- 1 small onion, finely chopped
- 1 stalk celery, finely diced
- 2 tablespoons chopped fresh parsley
- 15 ounces canned salmon, drained, or 1 1/2 cups cooked salmon
- 1 large egg, lightly beaten
- 1 ½ teaspoons Dijon mustard
- 1 3/4 cups fresh whole-wheat breadcrumbs, (see Tip)
- ½ teaspoon freshly ground pepper
- Creamy Dill Sauce (see Associated Recipe)
- 1 lemon, cut into wedges

Calories: 350
Fat: 14g
Carbs: 26g
Protein: 34g

PREPARATION

1. Set oven to 450 degrees Fahrenheit. Coat a large-rimmed baking sheet with cooking spray.
2. In a sizable nonstick skillet over medium-high heat, warm 1 1/2 teaspoons of oil. Add the onion and celery; simmer for about 3 minutes while stirring. After adding the parsley, turn off the heat.
3. In a medium bowl, put the salmon. With a fork, break apart; take off any skin and bones. Stir in the egg and mustard. Mix well after adding the breadcrumbs, onion mixture, and pepper.
4. Create 8 roughly 2 1/2-inch-wide patties out of the mixture.
5. In the pan, heat the remaining 1 1/2 tablespoons of oil. Add 4 patties and cook for 2 to 3 minutes, or until the undersides are brown.
6. Turn them over onto the prepared baking sheet using a wide spatula. The remaining patties should be repeated.
7. Bake the salmon cakes for 15 to 20 minutes, or until they are heated all the way through. Make the Creamy Dill Sauce in the meantime. Serve lemon wedges and sauce alongside the salmon cakes.

SWEET POTATO CARBONARA WITH SPINACH & MUSHROOMS

4 SERVINGS

DIFFICULT

COST

INGREDIENTS

- 2 pounds sweet potatoes, peeled
- 3 large eggs, beaten
- 1 cup grated Parmesan cheese
- ¼ teaspoon salt
- ¼ teaspoon ground pepper
- 1 tablespoon extra-virgin olive oil
- 3 strips center-cut bacon, chopped
- 1 ounce package sliced mushrooms
- 2 cloves garlic, minced
- 1 ounce package baby spinach

Calories: 312
Fat: 12g
Carbs: 38g
Protein: 15g

PREPARATION

1. Start the water in a big pot to boil.
2. Cut sweet potatoes lengthwise into long, thin strands using a spiral vegetable slicer or a julienne vegetable peeler.
3. Cook the sweet potatoes in the boiling water, gently stirring once or twice, for 1 1/2 to 3 minutes, or until they just begin to soften but are still slightly firm.
4. After draining, save 1/4 cup of the cooking water.
5. Off the heat, add the noodles back to the saucepan. In a bowl, whisk the eggs with the Parmesan, salt, pepper, and the conserved water.
6. Pour the mixture over the noodles and toss gently with tongs to coat.
7. Heat oil in a large skillet over medium heat. Add bacon and mushrooms and cook, stirring often, until the liquid has evaporated and the mushrooms are starting to brown, 6 to 8 minutes. Add garlic and cook, stirring, until fragrant, about 1 minute.
8. Add spinach and cook, stirring, until wilted, 1 to 2 minutes. Add the vegetables to the noodles and toss to combine.
9. Top with a generous grinding of pepper

CORIANDER-&-LEMON-CRUSTED SALMON WITH ASPARAGUS SALAD & POACHED EGG

4 SERVINGS

DIFFICULT

COST

INGREDIENTS

- 1 tablespoon coriander seeds
- 1 teaspoon lemon zest
- ¾ teaspoon fine sea salt, divided
- ½ teaspoon crushed red pepper
- 1 pound wild salmon (see Tips), skin-on, cut into 4 portions
- 1 pound asparagus, trimmed
- 2 tablespoons extra-virgin olive oil
- 1 tablespoon lemon juice
- 1 tablespoon chopped fresh mint
- 1 tablespoon chopped fresh tarragon
- ¼ teaspoon ground pepper, plus more for garnish
- 8 cups water
- 1 tablespoon white vinegar
- 4 large eggs

Calories: 288
Fat: 16g
Carbs: 14g
Protein: 26g

PREPARATION

1. Place a rack in the upper third of the oven and turn the broiler to high. Spray cooking oil on a baking sheet with a rim.
2. For about 3 minutes, while shaking the pan periodically over medium heat, toast the coriander until aromatic. Coriander, lemon zest, 1/2 teaspoon salt, and crushed red pepper should be finely minced in a spice grinder.
3. Place the salmon on the prepared baking sheet after coating the flesh with the spice mixture (approximately 1 1/2 tablespoons each part).
4. Trim asparagus's tips, then slice the stalks diagonally into very thin slices. Toss the tips and slices with the remaining 1/4 teaspoon salt, pepper, mint, lemon juice, and tarragon. While you prepare the eggs and salmon, let stand.
5. In a big pot, bring water and vinegar to a boil.
6. In the meantime, broil the salmon for 3 to 6 minutes, depending on thickness, until just cooked through. To stay warm, make a foil tent.
7. Bring the boiling water to a simmering boil. To get the water to swirl around the saucepan, gently whisk in a circle. Crack eggs into the water one at a time.
8. Cook for 3 to 4 minutes, or until the whites are set but the yolks are still runny.
9. Divide the salmon and asparagus salad among 4 dishes before serving. Create a nest in each salad and place an egg on top.

HAZELNUT-PARSLEY ROAST TILAPIA

4 SERVINGS

DIFFICULT

COST

INGREDIENTS

- 2 tablespoons olive oil, divided
- 4 (5 ounce) tilapia fillets (fresh or frozen, thawed)
- ⅓ cup finely chopped hazelnuts
- ¼ cup finely chopped fresh parsley
- 1 small shallot, minced
- 2 teaspoons lemon zest
- ⅛ teaspoon salt plus ¼ teaspoon, divided
- ¼ teaspoon ground pepper, divided
- 1 ½ tablespoons lemon juice

PREPARATION

1. Preheat oven to 450 degrees F. Line a large rimmed baking sheet with foil; brush with 1 Tbsp. oil. Bring fish to room temperature by letting it stand on the counter for 15 minutes.
2. Meanwhile, stir together hazelnuts, parsley, shallot, lemon zest, 1 tsp. oil, 1/8 tsp. salt, and 1/8 tsp. pepper in a small bowl.
3. Pat both sides of the fish dry with a paper towel. Place the fish on the prepared baking sheet. Brush both sides of the fish with lemon juice and the remaining 2 tsp. oil.
4. Season both sides evenly with the remaining 1/4 tsp. salt and 1/8 tsp. pepper. Divide the hazelnut mixture evenly among the tops of the fillets and pat gently to adhere.
5. Roast the fish until it is opaque, firm, and just beginning to flake, 7 to 10 minutes. Serve immediately.

Calories: 262
Fat: 15g
Carbs: 3g
Protein: 30g

MIXED VEGETABLE SALAD WITH LIME DRESSING

INGREDIENTS

- ¼ cup canola oil
- ¼ cup extra-virgin olive oil
- 3 tablespoons lime juice
- 1 ½ tablespoons finely chopped fresh cilantro
- ½ teaspoon salt
- ½ teaspoon ground pepper
- 2 cups mixed vegetables (steamed: sliced small red potatoes, carrots or beets, green beans, peas; raw: sliced radishes, cucumbers or tomatoes)
- 6 leaves romaine or leaf lettuce
- 1 small bunch watercress, large stems removed
- 1 hard-boiled large egg, sliced
- 1 thick slice red onion, broken into rings
- Crumbled Mexican queso fresco, feta or farmer's cheese for garnish

PREPARATION

1. In a medium bowl, stir together the canola and olive oils, lime juice, cilantro, salt, and pepper. A mixture of vegetables is added; toss to combine.
2. Line a large serving platter with lettuce. Place a serving dish on top of the prepared veggies. If preferred, top with egg, onion, and cheese after surrounding with watercress.

Calories: 214
Fat: 2g
Carbs: 28g
Protein: 6g

Snacks

APRICOT-SUNFLOWER GRANOLA BARS

INGREDIENTS

- 3 cups old-fashioned rolled oats
- 1 cup crispy brown rice cereal
- 1 cup finely chopped dried apricots (1/4 inch)
- ½ cup unsalted pepitas, toasted
- ½ cup unsalted sunflower seeds, toasted
- ¼ teaspoon salt
- ⅔ cup brown rice syrup or light corn syrup
- ½ cup sunflower seed butter
- 1 teaspoon ground cinnamon

Calories: 152
Fat: 6g
Carbs: 22g
Protein: 4g

PREPARATION

1. Set oven to 325 degrees Fahrenheit. Put parchment paper on the bottom and edges of a 9 by 13-inch baking pan, leaving some hanging over the sides. Spray some cooking spray on the parchment paper lightly.
2. In a sizable bowl, mix the oats, rice cereal, pepitas, sunflower seeds, and salt.
3. In a bowl that can be heated in the microwave, mix rice syrup (or corn syrup), sunflower butter, and cinnamon. 30 seconds in the microwave (or 1 minute in a saucepan over medium heat).
4. Stir to incorporate the addition with the dry ingredients. Use the back of a spatula to transfer to the prepared pan and press firmly into the pan.
5. For chewier bars, bake for 20 to 25 minutes, or until the edges are just beginning to color but the center is still soft. Bake for 30 to 35 minutes, or until the edges are golden brown and the centers are still somewhat gooey for crunchier bars. (Both remain soft when warm and become firmer as they cool.)
6. For easier lifting out of the pan onto a chopping board (it will still be soft), let cool in the pan for 10 minutes.
7. Cut into 24 bars, then allow to chill for a further 30 minutes without separating the bars. After cooling, cut into bars.

TRADITIONAL GREEK TAHINI DIP

INGREDIENTS

- ½ cup tahini
- 2 tablespoons lemon juice
- 1 tablespoon extra-virgin olive oil, plus more for garnish
- 1 clove garlic, crushed
- ¼ teaspoon salt
- 6 tablespoons water
- 3 tablespoons chopped fresh parsley
- Toasted sesame seeds for garnish

PREPARATION

1. Salt, garlic, oil, tahini, and lemon juice should all be combined in a food processor. As you pulse, scrape the sides as necessary to ensure smoothness.
2. Add water in a small stream while the motor is running until the mixture is smooth and light in color.
3. Place the dip in a bowl for serving and garnish with parsley.
4. Sesame seeds and more oil may be used as a garnish.

Calories: 106
Fat: 10g
Carbs: 9g
Protein: 3g

CHERRY-COCOA-PISTACHIO ENERGY BALLS

20 SERVINGS
DIFFICULT
COST

INGREDIENTS

- 1 ½ cups dried cherries
- ¾ cup shelled salted pistachios
- ½ cup almond butter
- 3 tablespoons cocoa powder
- 4 tablespoons pure maple syrup
- ½ teaspoon ground cinnamon

PREPARATION

1. In a food processor, mash cherries, pistachios, almond butter, cocoa powder, maple syrup, and cinnamon.
2. When the mixture is crumbly but can be squeezed into a cohesive ball, process for 10 to 20 pulses to finely chop the ingredients.
3. After that, process for about a minute, scraping down the sides as needed.
4. Squeeze about 1 tablespoon of the mixture firmly between your palms, then roll into a ball with wet hands (to stop the mixture from clinging to them). Place in a box for storage. The remaining mixture

Calories: 72
Fat: 4g
Carbs: 9g
Protein: 2g

AIR-FRYER SWEET POTATO CHIPS

8 SERVINGS
DIFFICULT
COST

INGREDIENTS

- 1 medium sweet potato, (about 8 ounces), sliced into 1/8-inch-thick rounds
- 1 tablespoon canola oil
- ¼ teaspoon sea salt
- ¼ teaspoon ground pepper

PREPARATION

1. Slices of sweet potato should be soaked for 20 minutes in a big bowl of cold water. Using paper towels, wipe the drain and dry.
2. Sweet potatoes should be put back in the dried dish. Salt, pepper, and oil to taste; gently toss to coat.
3. Spray some cooking spray on the air fryer basket lightly. Just enough sweet potatoes should be arranged in the basket to create one layer.
4. Cook for 15 minutes at 350 degrees F, rotating and rearranging into a single layer every 5 minutes, until well cooked and crispy.
5. Carefully transfer the chips from the air fryer to a platter using tongs. The remaining sweet potatoes should be repeated.
6. Serve the chips right away, or let them cool fully and store them in an airtight plastic container for up to three days. Let the chips cool for five minutes.

Calories: 123
Fat: 10g
Carbs: 19g
Protein: 11g

TUNA SALAD SPREAD

4 SERVINGS

DIFFICULT

COST

INGREDIENTS

- 1 avocado, mashed
- 2 tablespoons low-fat plain Greek yogurt
- 1 tablespoon lemon juice
- 1 tablespoon chopped fresh parsley
- ¼ teaspoon garlic powder
- ¼ teaspoon paprika
- ¼ teaspoon salt
- ¼ teaspoon ground pepper
- 1 (5 ounce) can albacore tuna in water, drained
- ¼ cup diced onion or celery

PREPARATION

1. In a small bowl, combine the avocado and yogurt and whisk well. Stir in the parsley, garlic powder, paprika, salt, and pepper after adding the lemon juice.
2. Mix gently until mixed after adding the tuna and onion (or celery).

Calories: 130
Fat: 8g
Carbs: 6g
Protein: 10g

KALE CHIPS

4 SERVINGS

DIFFICULT

COST

INGREDIENTS

- 1 large bunch kale, tough stems removed, leaves torn into pieces (about 16 cups)
- 1 tablespoon extra-virgin olive oil
- ¼ teaspoon salt

PREPARATION

1. Oven racks should be placed in the upper third and the center.
2. If the kale is moist, completely pat it dry with a clean dishtowel before transferring it to a large bowl.
3. Salt and oil should be drizzled over the kale. To uniformly distribute the oil and salt on the kale leaves, knead them with your hands.
4. Make careful to evenly distribute the kale leaves on 2 big rimmed baking pans. Make the chips in batches if all of the kale will not fit.
5. Bake for 8 to 12 minutes, rotating the pans from front to back and top to bottom halfway through, until the majority of the leaves are crisp. (If only using one baking sheet, check after 8 minutes to avoid scorching.)

Calories: 110
Fat: 5g
Carbs: 16g
Protein: 5g

24 SERVINGS

DIFFICULT

COST

VEGAN CHOCOLATE-DIPPED FROZEN BANANA BITES

INGREDIENTS

- 3 large bananas
- ¼ cup natural peanut butter (chunky or smooth)
- ¾ cup vegan chocolate chips

PREPARATION

1. Each peeled banana should be split lengthwise. Spread peanut butter on each half. Combine the banana halves to create banana "sandwiches." From each banana "sandwich," cut 8 rounds. Place the frozen banana pieces on a baking sheet or tray that has been lined with parchment paper or wax paper, and freeze for at least two hours or overnight.
2. Place chocolate chips in a microwave-safe bowl and microwave on High, in 15-second increments, until melted (1 to 1 1/2 minutes total). Each frozen banana bite is coated with chocolate on one half.
3. Let the chocolate stand until it has hardened. If not serving right away, put the food back in the freezer.

Calories: 58
Fat: 3g
Carbs: 8g
Protein: 1g

FRUIT ENERGY BALLS

24 SERVINGS

DIFFICULT

COST

INGREDIENTS

- 1 cup chopped almonds
- 1 cup dried figs
- 1 cup dried apricots
- ⅓ cup unsweetened shredded coconut

PREPARATION

1. Combine almonds, figs and apricots in a food processor; pulse until finely chopped.
2. Roll the mixture into small balls and dredge in coconut

Calories: 70
Fat: 3g
Carbs: 10g
Protein: 2g

ROASTED BEET HUMMUS

INGREDIENTS

- 1 (15 ounce) can no-salt-added chickpeas, rinsed
- 8 ounces roasted beets, coarsely chopped and patted dry
- ¼ cup tahini
- ¼ cup extra-virgin olive oil
- ¼ cup lemon juice
- 1 clove garlic
- 1 teaspoon ground cumin
- ½ teaspoon salt

PREPARATION

1. In a food processor, combine chickpeas, beets, tahini, oil, lemon juice, garlic, cumin, and salt.
2. Puree for 2 to 3 minutes, or until very smooth. Serve with crudités, pita chips, or vegetable chips.

Calories: 133
Fat: 10g
Carbs: 10g
Protein: 3g

AIR-FRYER CRISPY CHICKPEAS

INGREDIENTS

- 1 (15 ounce) can unsalted chickpeas, rinsed and drained
- 1 ½ tablespoons toasted sesame oil
- ¼ teaspoon smoked paprika
- ¼ teaspoon crushed red pepper
- ⅛ teaspoon salt
- Cooking spray
- 2 lime wedges

PREPARATION

1. On multiple layers of paper towels, spread the chickpeas. Roll the chickpeas beneath the paper towels to dry them on all sides, then add additional paper towels on top and pat until extremely dry.
2. Combine the chickpeas and oil in a medium bowl. Salt, crushed red pepper, and paprika should be added.
3. Pour into a cooking spray-coated air fryer basket. Cook for 12 to 14 minutes at 400 degrees F, shaking the basket occasionally, until very nicely browned.
4. Serve the chickpeas with lime wedges on top.

Calories: 132
Fat: 6g
Carbs: 14g
Protein: 5g

HOMEMADE TRAIL MIX

5 SERVINGS

DIFFICULT

COST

INGREDIENTS

- ¼ cup whole shelled (unpeeled) almonds
- ¼ cup unsalted dry-roasted peanuts
- ¼ cup dried cranberries
- ¼ cup chopped pitted dates
- 2 ounces dried apricots, or other dried fruit

PREPARATION

1. Combine almonds, peanuts, cranberries, dates and apricots (or other fruit) in a medium bowl.

Calories: 132
Fat: 7g
Carbs: 15g
Protein: 4g

ROASTED BUFFALO CHICKPEAS

4 SERVINGS

DIFFICULT

COST

INGREDIENTS

- 1 tablespoon white vinegar
- ½ teaspoon cayenne pepper, or to taste
- ¼ teaspoon salt
- 1 (15 ounce) can no-salt-added chickpeas, rinsed

PREPARATION

1. Oven rack should be in the upper third; heat to 400 degrees F.
2. Salt, cayenne, and vinegar are combined in a sizable basin. Chickpeas should be dried very completely before being mixed with the vinegar mixture.
3. Spread on a baking sheet with a rim. For 30 to 35 minutes, roast the chickpeas, tossing twice, until they are crisp and golden. The chickpeas will become crisp as they cool; leave to cool for 30 minutes on the pan.

Calories: 109
Fat: 1g
Carbs: 18g
Protein: 6g

AVOCADO HUMMUS

10 SERVINGS · **DIFFICULT** · **COST**

INGREDIENTS

- 1 (15 ounce) can no-salt-added chickpeas
- 1 ripe avocado, halved and pitted
- 1 cup fresh cilantro leaves
- ¼ cup tahini
- ¼ cup extra-virgin olive oil
- ¼ cup lemon juice
- 1 clove garlic
- 1 teaspoon ground cumin
- ½ teaspoon salt

PREPARATION

1. Chickpeas should be drained, with 2 tablespoons of the liquid saved.
2. Add the chickpeas and the liquid you set aside to a food processor. Avocado, cilantro, tahini, oil, lemon juice, garlic, cumin, and salt should all be added until very smooth, puree.
3. Serve with crudités, pita chips, or vegetable chips.

Calories: 156
Fat: 12g
Carbs: 10g
Protein: 3g

BEET CHIPS

5 SERVINGS
DIFFICULT
COST

INGREDIENTS

- 2 large beets (about 1 pound), thinly sliced (about 1/8 inch thick)
- 1 tablespoon extra-virgin olive oil
- ½ teaspoon salt

PREPARATION

1. Oven to 200 degrees Fahrenheit. 2 big baking sheets should be lined with parchment paper.
2. Slices of beet are tossed with salt and oil. Place on the preheated baking sheets in a single layer.
3. Bake for about three hours, turning the pans top to bottom and front to back, on the upper and lower oven racks, until crisp. Before serving, let the pans cool for 30 minutes.

Calories: 33
Fat: 2g
Carbs: 13g
Protein: 3g

BANANA ENERGY BITES

INGREDIENTS

- 1 overripe banana
- 1 cup dry quick-cooking rolled oats
- ½ cup roasted and salted pumpkin seeds (pepitas)
- ½ cup dried cranberries
- ½ cup natural peanut butter
- ¼ cup miniature semisweet chocolate pieces

PREPARATION

1. With a fork, mash the banana in a medium bowl until it is smooth. Oats, pumpkin seeds, dried cranberries, peanut butter, and chocolate chunks should all be stirred in.
2. Shape the mixture into 32 balls, using 1 tbsp for each bite; gently flatten.
3. Up to serving time, chill.

Calories: 145
Fat: 9g
Carbs: 14g
Protein: 5g

Dessert

WINE-POACHED PEARS

4 SERVINGS
DIFFICULT
COST

INGREDIENTS

- 2 cups dry red wine (such as Cabernet, Pinot Noir, or Merlot)
- 5 tablespoons sugar
- 1/2 cup orange juice
- 1 to 2 tablespoons orange zest
- 1 cinnamon stick
- 2 whole cloves
- 4 firm, ripe pears, free of blemishes, peeled, stems intact
- Vanilla Greek yogurt (optional)
- Toasted almond slices (optional)
- Fresh mint (optional)

PREPARATION

1. Wine, sugar, orange juice, orange zest, cinnamon stick, and cloves should all be combined in a 4-quart saucepan. Stir the sugar until it melts.
2. Bring the liquid to a boil before adding the pears. Once the pears are uniformly colored and soft, simmer them for 15 to 20 minutes with the lid on, turning them every five minutes.
3. The peaches should be placed in a dish to cool. After removing the cinnamon and cloves, boil the liquid for another 15 to 20 minutes, or until it has thickened and reduced by half.
4. A few teaspoons of the warm syrup should be drizzled over the pears when they are ready to be served, whether warm or at room temperature. If desired, garnish with a dollop of Greek yogurt, sliced almonds, and fresh mint.

Calories: 245
Fat: 2g
Carbs: 44g
Protein: 6g

4 SERVINGS

DIFFICULT

COST

STRAWBERRIES WITH PEPPERED BALSAMIC DRIZZLE

INGREDIENTS

- 2 cups fresh strawberries, washed and cut in half
- 1 tablespoon balsamic vinegar
- 1 tablespoon brown sugar
- Pinch freshly and finely ground black pepper
- 4 ounces vanilla Greek yogurt
- Fresh mint, for garnish

PREPARATION

1. Strawberries, balsamic vinegar, sugar, and pepper should all be combined in a bowl. To make sure the berries are evenly coated, gently stir.
2. For one hour, cover and leave at room temperature; after that, chill until ready to serve.
3. Add a dollop of yogurt on top after evenly distributing the strawberries across the four dishes.
4. Serve after adding a fresh mint leaf to the garnish.

Calories: 65
Fat: 2g
Carbs: 16g
Protein: 6g

VANILLA CHIA SEED PUDDING WITH TOPPINGS

INGREDIENTS

- 1 cup vanilla Greek yogurt
- 2 cups reduced-fat 2 percent milk
- 1/2 cup chia seeds
- 1-1/2 tablespoons maple syrup
- 1/2 teaspoon vanilla extract
- Pinch salt

PREPARATION

1. Whisk the yogurt, milk, chia seeds, maple syrup, vanilla, and salt until well combined in a large bowl.
2. Overnight or for three to four hours, cover and chill. If necessary, whisk the mixture one more just before serving to remove any clumps that may have developed.
3. Place in dessert cups and decorate with your preferred garnishes.

Calories: 92
Fat: 4g
Carbs: 10g
Protein: 6g

MANGO BANANA SOFT SERVE

6 SERVINGS

DIFFICULT

COST

INGREDIENTS

- 1 large ripe banana
- One 16-ounce package frozen mango chunks
- 1 to 2 tablespoons sugar
- 1-1/2 tablespoons lime juice
- 1-1/2 tablespoons canned light coconut milk
- Mint leaves, for garnish

PREPARATION

1. Bananas should be peeled, sliced in half, placed in a freezer bag that can be sealed, and frozen for at least four hours or until solid.
2. Mango and sugar should be combined in a sizable basin and left to stand for 5 minutes. (Skip the sugar if you'd like a little more acidity.)
3. Use the tamper to scrape down the sides of the high-speed blender as you pulse the mango, banana, lime juice, and coconut milk for 3 to 4 minutes, or until the mixture is thick and smooth.
4. For a softer consistency, scoop the soft serve into bowls and serve right away; otherwise, freeze until ready to serve. If desired, add mint leaves as a garnish.

Calories: 92
Fat: 4g
Carbs: 21g
Protein: 6g

°F	°C
50	10
100	37
150	65
200	93
250	121
300	150
350	176
400	204
450	232

US	EU
1 teaspoon	5 gr
1 tablespoon	15 gr
1 cup	250 gr
1/2 cup	125 gr
1 oz	30 gr
10 oz	315 gr
1 pound	16 oz/454 gr
1 cup	16 tablespoon
1 tablespoon	3 teaspoon

If you like the book, don't forget to let me know by scanning the following QR code and writing your review.

Thank you!

35 DAYS MEAL PLAN

WEEK 1

Monday

Berry-Almond Smoothie Bowl	BREAKFAST
Veggie & Hummus Sandwich	LUNCH
Smoked Salmon Salad Nicoise	DINNER
Kale Chips	EXTRA

Tuesday

Spinach-Avocado Smoothie	BREAKFAST
Spinach & Strawberry Meal-Prep Salad	LUNCH
Sweet Potato, Kale & Chicken Salad	DINNER
Fruit Energy Balls	EXTRA

Wednesday

Cantaloupe Smoothie	BREAKFAST
Smoked Salmon Salad Nicoise	LUNCH
Meal-Prep Vegan Lettuce Wraps	DINNER
Roasted Beet Hummus	EXTRA

Thursday

Vegan Smoothie Bowl	BREAKFAST
Winter Kale & Quinoa Salad with Avocado	LUNCH
Slow-Cooker Chicken Soup	DINNER
Air-Fryer Crispy Chickpeas	EXTRA

Friday

White Bean & Avocado Toast	BREAKFAST
Roasted Root Vegetables...	LUNCH
Winter Kale & Quinoa Salad with Avocado	DINNER
Avocado Hummus	EXTRA

Saturday

Mango-Ginger Smoothie	BREAKFAST
Eggplant Parmesan	LUNCH
Chicken & Vegetable Penne	DINNER
Homemade Trail Mix	EXTRA

Sunday

Peanut Butter Banana Toast	BREAKFAST
Chicken & Vegetable penne...	LUNCH
Dijon Salmon with Green Bean Pilaf	DINNER
Roasted Buffalo Chickpeas	EXTRA

Notes

THIS IS A SUGGESTION ON HOW TO COMBINE MEALS, CREATE YOUR OWN PLAN TOO...

WEEK 2

Monday

Chocolate-Banana Protein Smoothie	BREAKFAST
Sweet Potato, Kale & Chicken Salad	LUNCH
Smoked Salmon Salad Nicoise	DINNER
Air-Fryer Sweet Potato Chips	EXTRA

Tuesday

Raspberry Yogurt Cereal Bowl	BREAKFAST
Mason Jar Power Salad	LUNCH
Creamy Lemon Pasta with Shrimp	DINNER
Vegan Chocolate Dipped Frozen Banana Bites	EXTRA

Wednesday

Spinach & Egg Tacos	BREAKFAST
Walnut-Rosemary Crusted Salmon	LUNCH
Slow-Cooker Vegetarian Bolognese	DINNER
Strawberries with Peppered Balsamic Drizzle	EXTRA

Thursday

White Bean & Avocado Toast	BREAKFAST
Hasselback Eggplant Parmesan	LUNCH
Slow-Cooker Chicken Soup	DINNER
Mango Banana Soft Serve	EXTRA

Friday

Sheet-pan Chicken with Roasted...	BREAKFAST
Roasted Root Vegetables...	LUNCH
Salmon Couscous Salad	DINNER
Vanilla Chia Seed Pudding with Toppings	EXTRA

Saturday

Spinach-Avocado Smoothie	BREAKFAST
Chicken Caesar Pasta Salad	LUNCH
Slow-Cooker Chicken & Orzo...	DINNER
Wine-Poached Pears	EXTRA

Sunday

Vegan Smoothie Bowl	BREAKFAST
Slow-Cooker Vegetarian Bolognese	LUNCH
Fig & Goat Cheese Salad	DINNER
Homemade Trail Mix	EXTRA

Notes

WEEK 3

Monday

Pineapple Green Smoothie — BREAKFAST

Spinach & Strawberry Meal-Prep Salad — LUNCH

Eggplant Parmesan — DINNER

Kale Chips — EXTRA

Tuesday

Chocolate-Banana Protein Smoothie — BREAKFAST

Mason Jar Power Salad — LUNCH

Chicken-Quinoa Bowl with Olives & Cucumber — DINNER

Vegan Chocolate Dipped Frozen Banana Bites — EXTRA

Wednesday

Fruit & Yogurt Smoothie — BREAKFAST

Smoked Salmon Salad Nicoise — LUNCH

Slow-Cooker Vegetarian Bolognese — DINNER

Air-Fryer Crispy Chickpeas — EXTRA

Thursday

White Bean & Avocado Toast — BREAKFAST

Meal-Prep Vegan Lettuce Wraps — LUNCH

Chicken Caesar Pasta Salad — DINNER

Beet Chips — EXTRA

Friday

Vegan Smoothie Bowl — BREAKFAST

Salad with Chickpeas & Tuna — LUNCH

Slow-Cooker Vegetarian Bolognese — DINNER

Wine-Poached Pears — EXTRA

Saturday

Vegan Smoothie Bowl — BREAKFAST

Vegan Superfood Grain Bowls — LUNCH

Creamy Lemon Pasta with Shrimp — DINNER

Roasted Beet Hummus — EXTRA

Sunday

Peanut Butter-Banana Cinnamon Toast — BREAKFAST

Slow-Cooker Chicken & Chickpea Soup — LUNCH

Dijon Salmon with Green Bean Pilaf — DINNER

Homemade Trail Mix — EXTRA

Notes

WEEK 4

Monday

Meal-Prep Vegan Lettuce Wraps	BREAKFAST
Cauliflower Taco Bowls	LUNCH
Salmon & Asparagus	DINNER
Kale Chips	EXTRA

Tuesday

Spinach & Egg Scramble	BREAKFAST
Smoked Salmon Salad Nicoise	LUNCH
Chicken Pesto Pasta with Asparagus	DINNER
Wine-Poached Pears	EXTRA

Wednesday

Spinach & Egg Tacos	BREAKFAST
Smoked Salmon Salad Nicoise	LUNCH
Carbonara with Spinach & Mushrooms	DINNER
Beet Chips	EXTRA

Thursday

Really Green Smoothie	BREAKFAST
Veggie & Hummus Sandwich	LUNCH
Fig & Goat Cheese Salad	DINNER
Banana Energy Bites	EXTRA

Friday

Fruit & Yogurt Smoothie	BREAKFAST
Cauliflower Taco Bowls	LUNCH
Easy Salmon Cakes	DINNER
Roasted Buffalo Chickpeas	EXTRA

Saturday

Mango-Ginger Smoothie	BREAKFAST
Vegan Superfood Grain Bowls	LUNCH
Carbonara with Spinach & Mushrooms	DINNER
Air-Fryer Crispy Chickpeas	EXTRA

Sunday

Vegan Smoothie Bowl	BREAKFAST
Vegan Superfood Grain Bowls	LUNCH
Salmon with Asparagus	DINNER
Strawberries with Peppered Balsamic Drizzle	EXTRA

Notes

WEEK 5

Monday
Fruit & Yogurt Smoothie	BREAKFAST PG. 46
Cauliflower Taco Bowls	LUNCH PG. 55
Fig & Goat Cheese Salad	DINNER PG. 83
Kale Chips	EXTRA PG. 96

Tuesday
Really Green Smoothie	BREAKFAST PG. 45
Vegan Superfood Grain Bowls	LUNCH PG. 63
Chicken Pesto Pasta with Asparagus	DINNER PG. 84
Air-Fryer Crispy Chickpeas	EXTRA PG. 100

Wednesday
Vegan Smoothie Bowl	BREAKFAST PG. 50
Vegan Superfood Grain Bowls	LUNCH PG. 63
Carbonara with Spinach & Mushrooms	DINNER PG. 86
Beet Chips	EXTRA PG. 104

Thursday
Mango-Ginger Smoothie	BREAKFAST PG. 48
Veggie & Hummus Sandwich	LUNCH PG. 56
Easy Salmon Cakes	DINNER PG. 85
Wine-Poached Pears	EXTRA PG. 107

Friday
Meal-Prep Vegan Lettuce Wraps	BREAKFAST PG. 60
Smoked Salmon Salad Nicoise	LUNCH PG. 58
Salmon with Asparagus	DINNER PG. 87
Strawberries with Peppered Balsamic Drizzle	EXTRA PG. 108

Saturday
Spinach & Egg Tacos	BREAKFAST PG. 44
Cauliflower Taco Bowls	LUNCH PG. 55
Carbonara with Spinach & Mushrooms	DINNER PG. 86
Banana Energy Bites	EXTRA PG. 105

Sunday
Spinach & Egg Scramble	BREAKFAST PG. 40
Smoked Salmon Salad Nicoise	LUNCH PG. 58
Salmon & Asparagus	DINNER PG. 81
Roasted Buffalo Chickpeas	EXTRA PG. 102

Notes

LOW-FODMAP DIET COOKBOOK

FIND OUT HOW TO IMPROVE YOUR QUALITY OF LIFE BY REDUCING THE IMPACT OF IBS AND OTHER GASTROINTESTINAL PROBLEMS WITH 100+ DELICIOUS AND HEALTHFUL DISHES TO BOOST DIGESTIVE HEALTH

Robert Kevin Edwards

IMPORTANT, READ CAREFULLY - MEDICAL DISCLAIMER

This book is provided for educational and informational purposes only and does not constitute the provision of medical advice. The information provided should not be used to diagnose or treat any health problem or disease, and individuals seeking personal medical advice should consult a licensed physician.

Always seek the advice of your doctor or another qualified healthcare professional regarding any medical condition. Never ignore professional medical advice or delay seeking it because of something you have read in this book. Before using the food recipes in this book, it is advisable to consult a physician to ensure they are appropriate for your personal physical condition.

CHAPTER 1: UNDERSTANDING DIGESTIVE DISTRESS......................140

CHAPTER 2: THE GUT MICROBIOME 142

CHAPTER 3: FODMAPS UNVEILED..145

CHAPTER 4: PREPARING FOR YOUR JOURNEY 16

CHAPTER 5: THE ELIMINATION PHASE 19

CHAPTER 6: THE REINTRODUCTION PHASE......................................153

CHAPTER 7: THE 8 TIPS YOU MUST ABSOLUTELY FOLLOW 156

CHAPTER 8: A FODMAP-FRIENDLY LIFESTYLE 160

CHAPTER 9: ENHANCING GUT HEALTH FOR LONG-TERM DIGESTIVE

WELL-BEING...163

BREAKFAST 167

SCRAMBLED EGGS WITH TOMATOES AND AVOCADO.......................... 168

GLUTEN-FREE YOGURT PARFAIT WITH LOW FODMAP FRUITS AND GRANOLA . 168

GLUTEN-FREE TOAST WITH PEANUT BUTTER AND BANANA 169

BREAKFAST SMOOTHIE WITH LOW FODMAP FRUITS, SPINACH, AND ALMOND

MILK 169

GLUTEN-FREE OATMEAL WITH STRAWBERRIES AND ALMOND BUTTER 170

RICE CAKE WITH TUNA AND CUCUMBER...170

BREAKFAST BURRITO WITH SCRAMBLED EGGS, PEPPERS, AND BACON 170

CHIA SEED PUDDING WITH LOW FODMAP FRUITS AND COCONUT MILK 171

GLUTEN-FREE GRANOLA WITH YOGURT AND LOW FODMAP FRUITS 172

BREAKFAST HASH WITH SWEET POTATOES, PEPPERS, AND SAUSAGE..............172

GLUTEN-FREE PANCAKES WITH BLUEBERRIES AND MAPLE SYRUP 173

SHAKSHUKA WITH TOMATO, BELL PEPPER, AND EGGS......................................174

CHIA SEED PUDDING WITH LOW FODMAP FRUITS AND COCONUT MILK 174

GLUTEN-FREE WAFFLES WITH STRAWBERRIES AND CREAM.............................175

QUINOA BREAKFAST BOWL WITH SCRAMBLED EGGS AND AVOCADO 176

AVOCADO AND QUINOA BREAKFAST BOWL..176

BREAKFAST SANDWICH WITH GLUTEN-FREE BREAD, EGG, AND BACON 177

GLUTEN-FREE OATMEAL WITH RASPBERRIES AND ALMONDS 178

SCRAMBLED EGGS WITH SPINACH AND TOMATO...178

BANANA AND BLUEBERRY SMOOTHIE...179

PEANUT BUTTER AND BANANA RICE CAKES...179

OMELETTE WITH SPINACH AND FETA...179

QUINOA BREAKFAST BOWL 180

BLUEBERRY PANCAKES 180

CHIA SEED PUDDING 181

GREEK YOGURT PARFAIT 181

RICE CAKE WITH SMOKED SALMON 181

VEGGIE AND BACON FRITTATA..182

PEANUT BUTTER BANANA SMOOTHIE BOWL..182

VEGGIE BREAKFAST BURRITO 183

RASPBERRY CHIA SEED PUDDING 183

SPINACH AND FETA WRAP..184

LOW-FODMAP PANCAKES 184

BACON AND TOMATO OMELETTE.. 185

STRAWBERRY AND ALMOND BUTTER TOAST 185

BREAKFAST QUICHE WITH SPINACH AND BACON............................. 186

MIXED BERRY OVERNIGHT OATS 186

TOFU SCRAMBLE WITH SPINACH AND TOMATOES 187

MEAT..188

GRILLED CHICKEN WITH ROASTED VEGETABLES............................. 189

TURKEY AND LETTUCE WRAP.. 189

LOW FODMAP CHICKEN AND VEGETABLE SKEWERS 190

CHICKEN AND VEGETABLE KEBABS WITH QUINOA.......................... 190

LOW FODMAP CHICKEN AND VEGETABLE STIR-FRY WITH RICE NOODLES 191

TURKEY AND POTATO HASH 192

LOW FODMAP CHICKEN CAESAR SALAD 192

LOW FODMAP CHICKEN AND VEGETABLE SKEWERS WITH QUINOA 193

TURKEY LETTUCE WRAPS WITH LOW FODMAP DIPPING SAUCE 194

TURKEY AND SPINACH STUFFED BELL PEPPERS 195

ROASTED LEMON HERB CHICKEN THIGHS 195

PORK TENDERLOIN WITH MAPLE GLAZE.. 196

TURKEY AND CRANBERRY STUFFED ACORN SQUASH 196

GREEK SALAD WITH GRILLED CHICKEN 197

GRILLED CHICKEN WITH LOW FODMAP VEGETABLES AND BROWN RICE.......... 197

CHICKEN AND VEGETABLE STIR-FRY... 198

CHICKEN AND VEGETABLE KABOBS WITH BROWN RICE 198

LOW FODMAP CHICKEN AND VEGETABLE STIR-FRY WITH QUINOA 199

GRILLED PORK TENDERLOIN WITH ROASTED CARROTS AND PARSNIPS 200

LEMON HERB ROASTED CHICKEN WITH GREEN BEANS 201

LOW FODMAP BEEF AND BROCCOLI STIR-FRY WITH RICE NOODLES................. 201

PAN-SEARED SCALLOPS WITH ROASTED BRUSSELS SPROUTS AND SWEET POTATO MASH 202

HERB MARINATED LAMB CHOPS WITH GRILLED EGGPLANT AND RED PEPPER .203

TOMATO BASIL CHICKEN 204

LOW FODMAP SPAGHETTI SQUASH WITH TURKEY MEATBALLS AND TOMATO SAUCE 204

GRILLED LEMON HERB CHICKEN..205

TURKEY AND CRANBERRY LETTUCE WRAPS 205

FISH 207

CILANTRO LIME GRILLED FISH WITH ROASTED CAULIFLOWER AND QUINOA 208

BAKED SWEET POTATO WITH LOW FODMAP TUNA SALAD 208

LOW FODMAP TUNA AND AVOCADO SALAD.....................................209

SHRIMP AND AVOCADO SALAD 209

GRILLED SALMON WITH ROASTED VEGETABLES 79

GRILLED SHRIMP WITH QUINOA SALAD 211

BAKED COD WITH LEMON AND HERBS...212

TERIYAKI GLAZED SALMON 212

LEMON HERB SALMON SALAD..213

TUNA SALAD LETTUCE WRAPS..213

GRILLED SALMON WITH ROASTED SWEET POTATO 214

BAKED SALMON WITH DILL SAUCE 214

GRILLED SHRIMP AND VEGETABLE SKEWERS 215

LEMON GARLIC SHRIMP SCAMPI 215

SALMON AND DILL ZUCCHINI NOODLES..216

LOW FODMAP SUSHI ROLLS WITH CRAB AND CUCUMBER 216

VEGETABLES 218

QUINOA-STUFFED BELL PEPPERS 219

SPINACH AND FETA OMELETTE 219

QUINOA AND ROASTED VEGETABLE SALAD 220

GARLIC ROASTED SHRIMP WITH ASPARAGUS AND BROWN RICE 220

VEGETABLE RICE 221

BAKED SWEET POTATO 221

WITH LOW FODMAP TOPPINGS 222

LOW FODMAP ZUCCHINI AND TOMATO QUICHE 223

ROASTED BUTTERNUT SQUASH SOUP 223

TOMATO AND BASIL ZUCCHINI NOODLES 224

GRILLED ZUCCHINI AND EGGPLANT STACK 224

GRILLED LEMON GARLIC ASPARAGUS 224

SCRAMBLED EGGS WITH SPINACH AND TOMATO 225

CUCUMBERS AND TOMATOES SALAD 225

SPAGHETTI SQUASH WITH PESTO 226

ROASTED RED PEPPER AND TOMATO SOUP 226

BAKED TOFU WITH PEANUT SAUCE 227

DESSERT 228

BANANA AND BLUEBERRY SMOOTHIE BOWL 229

VANILLA ICE CREAM WITH FRESH STRAWBERRIES 229

CINNAMON-SPICED RICE PUDDING 230

FODMAP-FRIENDLY CHOCOLATE MOUSSE 230

LEMON BLUEBERRY PARFAIT 231

RASPBERRY ALMOND CHIA PUDDING 231

PINEAPPLE COCONUT SORBET 232

CHOCOLATE-DIPPED STRAWBERRIES 232

COCONUT RICE PUDDING WITH PASSION FRUIT 233

ALMOND AND RASPBERRY MINI TARTS...233

CONCLUSION 235

21-DAY FOOD PLAN...237

CHAPTER 1:

Understanding Digestive Distress

Contrary to popular belief, digestive issues are significantly more prevalent. These are medical conditions that have an impact on how well our digestive systems functions and can cause a number of unpleasant symptoms. The presence of digestive issues is not unusual. In actuality, they are rather typical. Worldwide, millions of people go through digestive system-related problems at some time in their lives. These difficulties might range in severity from little annoyance to more serious concerns that have a big influence on everyday living.

Age is no barrier for digestive issues. Anyone, from young toddlers to elderly people, can be impacted. While certain digestive issues may start as a kid and persist throughout maturity, others may appear later in life. This means that everyone should be concerned about their gut health. A person's quality of life may be significantly impacted by digestive issues. Constipation, diarrhea, and stomach discomfort are just a few examples of symptoms that can be emotionally upsetting in addition to being physically painful. They have the power to restrict activities that individuals find pleasurable, such as going out with friends, indulging in their preferred meals, or engaging in hobbies.

A RANGE OF SYMPTOMS

Different symptoms might appear in people with digestive issues. While some people cope with regular diarrhea, others may have chronic constipation. Some people could have both at various points. Other typical symptoms include pains in the abdomen, bloating, and gas. Because there are so many different symptoms, no two people's experiences with digestive issues are precisely the same.

It's important to seek medical attention when dealing with chronic or severe symptoms of digestive issues due to their prevalence and effects. While occasional moderate digestive discomfort is common, persistent or serious problems should not be disregarded. Doctors and gastroenterologists are qualified healthcare specialists who can identify and manage these illnesses.

The first step in resolving these problems is realizing how common digestive ailments are. We can better understand the need for practical solutions, like the Low FODMAP Diet, to enhance digestive health and general well-being by being aware that these issues are widespread and can impact people of all ages. Recognizing the significance of these disorders and adopting proactive measures to control them is the first step on the path to digestive wellness.

CHAPTER 2:

The Gut Microbiome

Your digestive system, namely the colon, is home to the gut microbiome, sometimes referred to as your "gut flora," which is a teeming community of billions of bacteria. This tiny population consists of microorganisms including bacteria, viruses, fungi, and other germs. They are necessary to maintain overall health, which includes digestive health.

Complex carbohydrates and other nutrients that your body cannot absorb on its own are aided to be broken down and fermented by your gut flora. As a result of this process, short-chain fatty acids and other chemicals are produced, which your body may use for energy and other essential functions.

Immune Mechanism A healthy gut microbiota controls the function of your immune system. It impacts how your body responds to illnesses and infections and works as a protection against harmful bacteria.

Mental and Mood Health Unexpectedly, your stomach and brain are linked by a complex network known as the gut-brain axis. Your gut microbiome may alter, which may have an impact on your stress levels, mood, and even mental health conditions like melancholy and anxiety.

Your diet plays a significant role in shaping the composition and well-being of your gut microbiota. What you eat directly influences which bacteria thrive in your gut and which ones struggle to survive. Here are several ways in which diet impacts the gut microbiota:

High-fiber foods, such as fruits, vegetables, whole grains, and legumes, are essential for nourishing the beneficial bacteria in the gut. These foods, often referred to as prebiotics, contain fiber that supports the growth of advantageous gut microbes.

Probiotics, found in foods like yogurt, kefir, and fermented vegetables, introduce live beneficial bacteria into the gut, promoting the development of a diverse gut microbiota. The type of dietary fat you consume, particularly saturated fats, can influence the types of bacteria present in your gut.

Artificial sweeteners, including saccharin and aspartame, have been associated with changes in gut flora, although the impact of these changes may not always be beneficial.

Further research is needed to fully understand how various dietary preservatives and additives affect gut health.

It's essential to have a healthy gut flora for overall wellness. Here are a few strategies to promote a balanced gut microbiome

Consume a Range of Foods Consuming a wide variety of meals, such as fruits, vegetables, healthy grains, and lean meats, may help to promote a diverse gut flora.

Fiber-rich foods should always come first since they provide essential nutrients for a healthy gut flora. Set a minimum daily fiber consumption target of 25 to 30 grams.

To add good bacteria into your diet, eat probiotic-rich foods like yogurt, kefir, sauerkraut, and kimchi.

Reduce your intake of artificial chemicals and highly processed foods since they may harm the bacteria in your stomach.

"Remain Hydrated" Drinking enough of water is necessary for maintaining the gut mucous membrane, which is essential for a healthy microbiota.

Avoid Using Antibiotics Excessively If you use antibiotics, your gut's microbiota may become unbalanced. Use them only in accordance with a doctor's advice and instructions. When people are aware of the vital role the gut microbiota plays in digestive health and how food may impact it, they are better able to make informed dietary decisions. Adopting a gut-friendly diet and lifestyle can help you support the balance and health of your gut bacteria, which will eventually enhance your digestive wellbeing.

CHAPTER 3:

Fodmaps Unveiled

Fermentable Oligosaccharides, Disaccharides, Monosaccharides, and Polyols, or FODMAPs, are a class of short-chain carbohydrates that are present in many meals. Let's define each of these concepts individually Fermentable The bacteria in your stomach may ferment FODMAPs, which are carbohydrates. This fermentation process may result in gas production, which can cause bloating and discomfort.

Oligosaccharides These are carbohydrates consisting of a few connected sugar molecules. FODMAPs mostly contain fructans and galactans, which are two different forms of oligosaccharides.

Disaccharides Disaccharides are carbohydrates that are created by joining two sugar molecules. This group of FODMAPs includes lactose.

Monosaccharides monosaccharides are Single sugar molecules, another FODMAP is fructose, which is a monosaccharide.

Polyols Some fruits and vegetables contain polyols, which are sugar alcohols. Sorbitol, mannitol, and xylitol are a few examples.

HOW FODMAPS CAUSE DIGESTIVE SYMPTOMS

Understanding how FODMAPs could result in gastrointestinal discomfort is critical

Fermentation FODMAPs are swiftly broken down by bacteria in the intestines. Gases like hydrogen and methane are produced as a result of this process, which results in gas and bloating.

Osmotic Effect The osmotic properties of FODMAPs may lead to water absorption in the intestines. This could result in diarrhea or loose stools.

FODMAPs have the capacity to trigger gut nerve endings, which may heighten gut sensitivity and pain, particularly in people who already have conditions like Irritable Bowel Syndrome (IBS).

COMMON FOODS' FODMAP CONTENT

Some wheat-based foods like bread and pasta, which are high in fructans, dairy products containing lactose (like milk and some cheeses), some fruits (like apples and pears), which are high in fructose, and sweeteners like sorbitol, mannitol, and xylitol are examples of foods high in FODMAPs.

Low FODMAP Foods Fortunately, there are a number of low FODMAP alternatives available. These consist of low FODMAP fruits like bananas and berries, as well as grains like rice and maize, dairy products devoid of lactose and gluten, and dairy products.

It's important to remember that the amount of FODMAPs in foods varies depending on the cuisine, and that portion sizes also vary. For individuals following a low FODMAP diet, understanding high and low FODMAP foods and paying attention to portion quantities are essential for managing gastrointestinal symptoms.

By understanding the nature of FODMAPs and how they interact with the digestive system, people may make informed dietary decisions and take action to lessen pain caused by digestive issues.

CHAPTER 4:
Preparing for Your Journey

Before starting your Low FODMAP Diet journey, it is essential to get professional counsel, ideally from a licensed dietitian or healthcare specialist. Here's why taking this action is essential

Personalization Everybody's digestive system and triggers are unique. A expert can help you tailor the diet to your unique needs and help you identify any FODMAP triggers that may affect you personally.

Accuracy Professionals can accurately assess your symptoms, medical history, and dietary habits to determine whether the Low FODMAP Diet is the right option for you. They can rule out further potential causes of abdominal pain.

Monitoring During the diet, it is possible to check your progress continuously with the help of a doctor or nutritionist. They may make the necessary adjustments and provide guidance to make sure your nutritional and health requirements are met.

Avoiding nutritional deficiencies When you restrict certain foods, you may experience nutritional deficiencies. An expert can assist you in avoiding this. They can make relevant dietary modifications or supplementary recommendations.

PUTTING TOGETHER YOUR SUPPORT TEAM

With a supporting team by your side, starting the low FODMAP diet can be more bearable and less intimidating. You may want the following people on your support group

Registered Dietitian For nutritional advice, meal planning, and support throughout your journey, a registered dietitian with knowledge of the Low FODMAP Diet might be your best bet.

A primary care doctor or a gastroenterologist can help you identify and treat any underlying gastrointestinal disorders, offer medical advice, and make sure your diet is in line with your general health. Mental health expert Managing gastrointestinal distress can be emotionally difficult. If you experience stress, anxiety, or depression while on the diet, a mental health specialist can assist you in managing these emotions. Family and friends may offer you emotional support and understanding when it comes to preparing meals and social occasions if you let them know about your dietary limitations and goals.

SETTING REASONABLE EXPECTATIONS AND GOALS

Starting the low FODMAP diet might be more manageable and less daunting if you have a supportive group at your side. Consider include the following individuals in your support network

trained Dietitian A trained dietitian who is familiar with the Low FODMAP Diet may be your best choice for nutritional guidance, meal planning, and support during your journey.

You may get medical guidance from a primary care physician or a gastroenterologist, who can also assist you in identifying and treating any underlying gastrointestinal illnesses. They can also make sure your diet is in accordance with your overall health.

Managing gastrointestinal distress can be emotionally challenging, according to a mental health specialist. A mental health professional can help you manage your emotions if you feel stress, anxiety, or sadness while following the diet.

If you let your family and friends know about your dietary restrictions and objectives, they may be able to provide you with emotional support and understanding when it comes to cooking meals and attending social events.

CHAPTER 5:
The Elimination Phase

Before you start the Elimination Phase of the Low FODMAP Diet, it's essential to clear your pantry and kitchen of high FODMAP foods

Label Reading Familiarize yourself with food labels to identify high FODMAP ingredients. Look out for terms like "wheat," "onion," "garlic," "lactose," "high-fructose corn syrup," and "sorbitol."

Donate or Store Consider donating non-compliant foods to local food banks or temporarily storing them out of sight to reduce temptation.

Replace Staples Identify high FODMAP staples in your pantry, such as wheat flour, regular pasta, or onion-infused cooking oils. Replace them with low FODMAP alternatives like rice flour, gluten-free pasta, or garlic-infused oil (the oil is low FODMAP when the solid particles are strained out).
Check Sauces and Condiments Many sauces and condiments contain high FODMAP ingredients. Check the labels and opt for FODMAP-friendly versions or make your own.

A COMPREHENSIVE LIST OF FOODS TO AVOID

Understanding which foods to avoid during the Elimination Phase is crucial for symptom relief
High FODMAP Fruits Avoid fruits like apples, pears, cherries, and watermelon.

High FODMAP Vegetables Steer clear of onions, garlic, cauliflower, mushrooms, and snow peas.

High FODMAP Grains Eliminate wheat-based products, such as regular bread, pasta, and certain cereals.

High FODMAP Dairy Avoid milk, yogurt, and soft cheeses that contain lactose. Opt for lactose-free or non-dairy alternatives.

High FODMAP Legumes Say no to beans, lentils, and chickpeas.

High FODMAP Sweeteners Eliminate foods and drinks sweetened with high FODMAP sweeteners like high-fructose corn syrup, sorbitol, mannitol, and xylitol.

High FODMAP Sweet Fruits Exclude fruits like apples, pears, and mangoes from your diet.

Certain Nuts and Seeds Some nuts and seeds, like pistachios and cashews, are high FODMAP. Choose safe options like almonds and pumpkin seeds.

SMART SHOPPING FOR LOW FODMAP ALTERNATIVES

Navigating the grocery store during the Elimination Phase requires strategic shopping for low FODMAP alternatives

Read Labels Always read food labels to check for high FODMAP ingredients. Look for products labeled "FODMAP-friendly" or "low FODMAP" when available.

Gluten-Free Grains Opt for gluten-free grains like rice, quinoa, and oats (certified gluten-free). These are suitable alternatives to high FODMAP grains.

Lactose-Free Dairy Choose lactose-free milk, yogurt, and cheese options to replace high FODMAP dairy products.

Fresh Produce Stock up on low FODMAP fruits and vegetables, such as strawberries, blueberries, carrots, and zucchini.

Protein: Sources Include safe protein sources like poultry, fish, tofu, and eggs in your shopping list.

By clearing your pantry of high FODMAP culprits, adhering to a comprehensive list of foods to avoid, and adopting smart shopping strategies for low FODMAP alternatives, you'll be well-prepared to navigate the Elimination Phase of the Low FODMAP Diet with ease and effectiveness, aiming for symptom relief and improved digestive health.

CHAPTER 6:

The Reintroduction Phase

It's crucial to purge your cupboard and kitchen of high FODMAP items before beginning the Elimination Phase of the low FODMAP diet

Food Label Reading Become familiar with food labels to spot items that are high in FODMAPs. Severe caution should be exercised when using words like "wheat," "onion," "garlic," "lactose," "high-fructose corn syrup," and "sorbitol."

Donate or Store To lessen temptation, think about giving non-compliant foods to nearby food charities or temporarily keeping them out of sight.

Replace items in your cupboard that are high in FODMAPs, such as wheat flour, ordinary pasta, or cooking oils flavored with onions. Substitute low FODMAP items instead, such as rice flour, gluten-free pasta, or garlic-infused oil (oil is low FODMAP when the solid particles are squeezed out).

Examine Sauces and Condiments Many sauces and condiments have substances that are high in FODMAPs. Look for versions that are FODMAP-friendly on the labeling or design your own.

A COMPLETE LIST OF FOODS TO STEER CLEAR OF

For symptom alleviation during the Elimination Phase, it is essential to know which foods to avoid

Avoid fruits with a high FODMAP count, such as apples, pears, cherries, and melons.

Avoid onions, garlic, cauliflower, mushrooms, and snow peas since they are high in FODMAPs.

High FODMAP Grains Avoid foods containing wheat, including ordinary bread, pasta, and certain cereals.

Avoid dairy products high in FODMAPs such lactose-containing milk, yogurt, and soft cheeses. Choose lactose-free or nondairy substitutes.

Legumes high in FODMAPs Avoid beans, lentils, and chickpeas.

Avoid foods and beverages that include high FODMAP sweeteners such high-fructose corn syrup, sorbitol, mannitol, and xylitol.

Fruits with a high FODMAP count Avoid eating things like apples, pears, and mangoes.

Specific Nuts and Seeds Pistachios and cashews, for example, are high in FODMAP. Almonds and pumpkin seeds are great choices.

PURCHASING LOW FODMAP ALTERNATIVES WISELY

Shopping for low FODMAP substitutes strategically when in the Elimination Phase is necessary for grocery store navigation

Always read food labels to look for items high in FODMAPs. When available, search for items with the designations "FODMAP-friendly" or "low FODMAP".

Gluten-Free Grains Choose gluten-free grains like oats, quinoa, and rice that have received certification. These are acceptable substitutes for cereals with a high FODMAP content.

Lactose-Free Dairy Instead of high FODMAP dairy items, choose lactose-free milk, yogurt, and cheese.

Stock up on fresh produce that is low in FODMAPs, such as strawberries, blueberries, carrots, and zucchini.

Include safe sources of protein on your grocery list, such as poultry, fish, tofu, and eggs. Low FODMAP Sauces Seek for condiments and sauces devoid of high FODMAP components. During this time, tamari sauce, a gluten-free soy sauce, comes in helpful. You'll be well-prepared to navigate the Elimination Phase of the Low FODMAP Diet with ease and effectiveness, aiming for symptom relief and improved digestive health, by purging your pantry of high FODMAP culprits, adhering to a thorough list of foods to avoid, and adopting smart shopping strategies for low FODMAP alternatives.

CHAPTER 7:

The 8 Tips You Must Absolutely Follow

Certainly, let's delve into more detailed explanations for each of the 7 expert tips on managing IBS and other digestive issues:

Consult a Medical Professional

Seeking expert help is the first step toward properly controlling intestinal difficulties. Consult a gastroenterologist or a primary care physician if you are suffering from gastrointestinal issues. They can do a comprehensive assessment that includes a medical history, physical examination, and any required testing such as blood work, stool tests, and imaging. Because stomach symptoms might overlap with a variety of illnesses, an accurate diagnosis is critical, as is ruling out other medical disorders.

Dietary Alterations

- Dietary changes can have a substantial influence on digestive health. The low-FODMAP diet is one such technique. FODMAPs are fermentable carbohydrates present in a variety of meals that might cause digestive issues in those who are sensitive to them. However, it is critical to follow this diet under the supervision of a trained dietitian who specializes in gastrointestinal diseases. They can create a customised FODMAP strategy for you based on your individual triggers and sensitivities. Maintaining a comprehensive food diary can assist you in identifying troublesome items and tracking your dietary improvement.

Stress Reduction

- Stress contributes significantly to the exacerbation of digestive issues. The gut-brain link is well-established, and emotional stress can cause physical symptoms such as cramps, diarrhea, or constipation. It is critical to incorporate stress-reduction measures into your everyday routine. Mindfulness meditation, deep breathing techniques, progressive muscle relaxation, and yoga can all assist with stress management and stomach problems. Consistency in these routines can result in long-term digestive advantages.

Hydration is Critical

- Adequate hydration is essential for proper digestion. Water is involved in practically every stage of digestion, from food breakdown through waste passage through the intestines. Drinking adequate water (about 8-10 cups per day) can help you maintain good digestive function. Individual demands, however, may vary depending on factors such as climate, physical activity, and general health. Keep an eye on your water level, especially if you have diarrhea or heavy perspiration.

Physical Activity on a Regular Basis

- Regular physical activity has various health advantages, including better digestion. Physical activity can help promote bowel movements and alleviate constipation symptoms. Walking, running, swimming, or cycling can improve general well-being and help to a healthy digestive system. Before beginning or changing an exercise plan, talk with your healthcare professional, especially if you have specific health concerns or limits.

Medicines and supplements

- Medications and supplements may be prescribed to treat particular symptoms of digestive issues. Antispasmodic pharmaceuticals, for example, can assist relieve gastrointestinal cramps, while anti-diarrheal meds can help manage diarrhea. To treat constipation, laxatives may be administered. Probiotics, fiber supplements, and digestive enzymes are examples of dietary supplements that may be beneficial to digestive health. Their usage, however, should always be addressed and overseen by your healthcare professional to ensure that they are appropriate for your condition and circumstances.

Maintain Your Knowledge

- Staying up to date on the newest advancements in the field of digestive health allows you to actively engage in your own treatment. Maintain contact with credible information sources, such as medical publications, healthcare websites, and patient advocacy groups. Understanding the most recent research, treatment choices, and upcoming medicines can help you make educated treatment decisions. Consider joining support groups or online communities where others with comparable diseases may share their experiences and thoughts.

It's critical to remember that dealing with digestive disorders is a team effort between you and your healthcare team. Regular check-ins with your healthcare practitioner are critical for tracking your progress, changing treatment plans as required, and addressing any new problems or obstacles that may develop on your path to digestive wellness.

Control Fiber Consumption

Fiber is an important part of gut health. The amount and type of fiber you should ingest, however, will depend on your symptoms and condition. Insoluble fibers, for example, can assist avoid constipation, but soluble fibers may aid in diarrhea control. Consult your nutritionist or doctor to establish the appropriate amount and kind of fiber to include in your diet depending on your individual requirements. A sudden increase in fiber might temporarily aggravate symptoms, so it's best to include it gradually into your diet.

CHAPTER 8:
A FODMAP-Friendly Lifestyle

Safe and effective, the low-FODMAP diet can alleviate the symptoms of irritable bowel syndrome (IBS) and other digestive disorders. Nevertheless, sustaining a low-FODMAP lifestyle after the initial phases of elimination and reintroduction may prove to be quite difficult. Advice on how to navigate a FODMAP-friendly lifestyle is presented in this chapter. It encompasses strategies for managing social situations, recognizing concealed FODMAPs, modifying cooking and grocery purchasing routines, as well as establishing a network of support.

Handling Social Situations and Dining Out

Social situations and dining out can be a challenge for people following a low-FODMAP diet. Here are a few tips for making it easier:

- Plan ahead. If you know you'll be eating out, do some research on the restaurant's menu in advance. Many restaurants have online menus or social media pages that can help you identify low-FODMAP options.
- Be flexible. Don't be afraid to ask for modifications to dishes. For example, you can ask for a dish to be prepared without onions or garlic, or you can ask for a smaller portion of a high-FODMAP ingredient.
- Bring your own food. If you're really worried about finding low-FODMAP options, you can always bring your own food. This is a great option for potlucks or other events where you don't have a lot of control over the menu.
- Identifying and Managing Hidden FODMAPs

FODMAPs can be hidden in a variety of foods, including processed foods, restaurant dishes, and even some natural foods. Here are a few tips for identifying hidden FODMAPs:

- Read food labels carefully. Many processed foods contain hidden FODMAPs, such as onions, garlic, and wheat. Be sure to read food labels carefully and look for these ingredients.
- Ask questions. If you're not sure whether a food contains FODMAPs, don't be afraid to ask the restaurant or food manufacturer.
- Learn about the different types of FODMAPs. Once you understand the different types of FODMAPs, you'll be better equipped to identify them in foods.
- Adapting Cooking and Grocery Shopping Habits

Following a low-FODMAP diet can require some changes to your cooking and grocery shopping habits. Here are a few tips:

- Stock up on low-FODMAP ingredients. When you're first starting out, it's helpful to stock up on a variety of low-FODMAP ingredients. This will make it easier to prepare meals at home.
- Cook more at home. Cooking at home gives you more control over the ingredients in your food.
- Read food labels carefully. When you're grocery shopping, be sure to read food labels carefully and look for hidden FODMAPs.
- Building a Support System

Having a support system can make it easier to stick to a low-FODMAP diet. Here are a few tips for building a support system:

- Talk to your doctor or dietitian. Your doctor or dietitian can provide guidance and support as you follow a low-FODMAP diet.
- Connect with other people who are following a low-FODMAP diet. There are many online forums and support groups where you can connect with other people who are going through the same thing.
- Set realistic expectations. It takes time to adjust to a new diet. Don't get discouraged if you slip up occasionally. Just keep moving forward and you'll eventually reach your goals.

Navigating a FODMAP-friendly lifestyle can be challenging, but it's definitely possible. By following the tips in this chapter, you can make it easier to stick to your diet and improve your digestive health.

CHAPTER 9:
Enhancing Gut Health for
Long-Term Digestive Well-being

The low-FODMAP diet is a proven dietary approach for managing symptoms associated with irritable bowel syndrome (IBS) and other digestive disorders. While it effectively reduces the intake of Fermentable Oligosaccharides, Disaccharides, Monosaccharides, And Polyols (FODMAPs), which can trigger digestive discomfort, a comprehensive approach to gut health goes beyond dietary restrictions.

Nurturing a Healthy Gut Microbiome: The Role of Probiotics and Prebiotics

The human gut houses a vast community of trillions of microorganisms, collectively known as the gut microbiome. These microorganisms play a crucial role in digestion, nutrient absorption, immune function, and overall health. A healthy gut microbiome is characterized by a diverse and balanced population of bacteria. However, various factors, including diet, stress, and medications, can disrupt this balance, leading to gut dysbiosis.

Probiotics are live microorganisms that, when consumed in adequate amounts, can confer health benefits to the host. Studies have shown that probiotics can help restore gut balance, improve digestive function, strengthen the immune system, and reduce inflammation. Prebiotics, on the other hand, are non-digestible carbohydrates that serve as food for beneficial gut bacteria. They promote the growth and activity of probiotics, further enhancing gut health.

Incorporating probiotics and prebiotics into the diet can significantly contribute to long-term digestive well-being. Probiotic-rich foods include yogurt, kefir, tempeh, and kimchi. Prebiotic-rich foods include whole grains, fruits, vegetables, and legumes.

Managing Stress: A Pathway to Gut Health

Stress plays a significant role in gut health. Chronic stress can disrupt the gut microbiome, leading to an imbalance in beneficial and harmful bacteria. This imbalance can contribute to digestive symptoms such as bloating, diarrhea, and constipation.

Effective stress management techniques are essential for maintaining a healthy gut microbiome. Practices such as yoga, meditation, mindfulness, and deep breathing can help reduce stress levels, promote relaxation, and enhance overall well-being.

Sleep: A Cornerstone of Gut Health

Adequate sleep is crucial for maintaining gut health. During sleep, the body undergoes various processes that support digestive functions. Sufficient sleep allows the gut to rest and repair itself, promoting the growth of beneficial bacteria and reducing inflammation. Establishing regular sleep patterns, creating a relaxing bedtime routine, and avoiding caffeine and alcohol before bed can significantly improve sleep quality and contribute to gut health.

Regular Exercise: A Catalyst for Gut Wellness

Regular physical activity is essential for overall health, including gut health. Exercise promotes the growth of beneficial gut bacteria, increases blood flow to the digestive tract, and reduces inflammation. Aim for at least 30 minutes of moderate-intensity exercise most days of the week.

Relaxation Techniques: Taming the Gut-Brain Connection

The gut-brain axis is a complex bidirectional communication system between the gut and the brain. Stress, anxiety, and other psychological factors can trigger digestive symptoms through this pathway. Relaxation techniques such as yoga, meditation, and deep breathing can help reduce stress, improve mood, and enhance gut health by modulating the gut-brain axis.

Embrace a Holistic Approach

Achieving long-term digestive well-being requires a holistic approach that considers not only dietary modifications but also lifestyle factors that influence gut health. By incorporating probiotics, prebiotics, stress management techniques, adequate sleep, regular exercise, and relaxation practices, individuals can create a nurturing environment for their gut microbiome, leading to improved digestion, overall health, and enhanced quality of life.

The low-FODMAP diet serves as a valuable tool for managing IBS and other digestive disorders. However, a comprehensive approach to gut health extends beyond dietary restrictions. By nourishing the gut microbiome, managing stress, prioritizing sleep, engaging in regular exercise, and incorporating relaxation techniques, individuals can cultivate long-term digestive well-being and overall health.

It's crucial to remember that managing digestive issues is a collaborative effort between you and your healthcare team. Regular follow-up appointments with your healthcare provider are essential for monitoring your progress, adjusting treatment plans as needed, and addressing any new concerns or challenges that may arise on your journey to digestive wellness.

Note: The nutritional values of the dishes provided should be considered as indicative.

BREAKFAST

SCRAMBLED EGGS WITH TOMATOES AND AVOCADO

SERVINGS: 2
PREPARATION TIME: 10 minutes

INGREDIENTS

- 4 eggs
- 1 medium tomato, diced
- 1/2 avocado, diced
- 1 tablespoon garlic-infused oil
- Salt and pepper to taste

INSTRUCTIONS

1. Crack the eggs into a bowl and whisk until well combined.
2. Heat the garlic-infused oil in a nonstick skillet over medium heat.
3. Add the diced tomato to the skillet and sauté for 2-3 minutes or until the tomato is slightly softened.
4. Pour the eggs into the skillet with the tomato and stir gently.
5. Cook the eggs, stirring occasionally, until they are scrambled and cooked through, about 3-5 minutes.
6. Remove the skillet from the heat and stir in the diced avocado.
7. Season with salt and pepper to taste.
8. Serve the scrambled eggs hot.

Calories: 274 per serving
Carbs: 6g
Protein: 16g
Fat: 21g

GLUTEN-FREE YOGURT PARFAIT WITH LOW FODMAP FRUITS AND GRANOLA

SERVINGS: 1
PREPARATION TIME: 5 minutes

INGREDIENTS

- 1/2 cup gluten-free granola
- 1/2 cup lactose-free Greek yogurt
- 1/2 cup low FODMAP fruits (such as blueberries, raspberries, or strawberries)
- 1 tablespoon chia seeds (optional)

INSTRUCTIONS

1. In a small bowl or glass, layer the gluten-free granola, lactose-free Greek yogurt, and low FODMAP fruits.
2. Repeat the layering until you reach the top of the bowl or glass.
3. Top with chia seeds, if desired.
4. Serve immediately.

Calories: 340
Carbohydrates:: 47g
Protein:: 19 g
Fat:: 4 g
Note: may vary depending on the specific ingredients and brands used.

GLUTEN-FREE TOAST WITH PEANUT BUTTER AND BANANA

SERVINGS: 1
PREPARATION TIME: 5 minutes

INGREDIENTS
- 2 slices gluten-free bread
- 1 tablespoon peanut butter (check for no added FODMAP ingredients)
- 1 small ripe banana, sliced
- Optional a drizzle of honey (for sweetness)

INSTRUCTIONS
1. Toast the gluten-free bread slices until golden brown.
2. Spread the peanut butter evenly over each slice of toasted bread.
3. Place the sliced banana on top of the peanut butter on one slice of bread.
4. Drizzle a small amount of honey over the banana if desired.
5. Place the other slice of bread on top to make a sandwich.
6. Serve and enjoy!

Calories: 360
Carbohydrates: 59g
Protein: 11g
Fat: 12g

BREAKFAST SMOOTHIE WITH LOW FODMAP FRUITS, SPINACH, AND ALMOND MILK

SERVINGS: 1
PREPARATION TIME: 5 minutes

INGREDIENTS
- 1/2 cup low FODMAP fruits (such as strawberries, blueberries, or raspberries)
- 1 handful baby spinach leaves
- 1/2 banana
- 1 cup unsweetened almond milk
- 1 tablespoon chia seeds
- 1/4 teaspoon vanilla extract

INSTRUCTIONS
1. Add the low FODMAP fruits, baby spinach leaves, and banana to a blender.
2. Pour in the almond milk, chia seeds, and vanilla extract.
3. If desired, add a few ice cubes to the blender for a chilled smoothie.
4. Blend all the ingredients until smooth and well combined.
5. Pour the smoothie into a glass and serve immediately.

Calories: 187
Carbohydrates: 27g
Protein: 6g
Fat: 7g

GLUTEN-FREE OATMEAL WITH STRAWBERRIES AND ALMOND BUTTER

SERVINGS: 1
PREPARATION TIME: 10 minutes

INGREDIENTS
- 1/2 cup gluten-free rolled oats
- 1 cup water
- 1/2 cup sliced strawberries
- 1 tablespoon almond butter
- 1 teaspoon honey
- 1/2 teaspoon cinnamon

INSTRUCTIONS
1. In a small pot, bring 1 cup of water to a boil.
2. Add the gluten-free rolled oats to the boiling water and reduce the heat to low.
3. Cook the oats for 5-7 minutes, stirring occasionally, until they are thick and creamy.
4. Remove the pot from the heat and stir in the sliced strawberries, almond butter, honey, and cinnamon.
5. Serve the oatmeal in a bowl and top with additional sliced strawberries and a drizzle of almond butter, if desired.

Calories: 335
Carbohydrates: 45g
Protein: 9g
Fat: 14g

RICE CAKE WITH TUNA AND CUCUMBER

SERVINGS: 1
PREPARATION TIME: 5 minutes

INGREDIENTS
- 1 rice cake
- 1 can of tuna (in water), drained
- 2 tablespoons of mayonnaise
- 1/4 cup of chopped cucumber
- Salt and pepper to taste

INSTRUCTIONS
1. In a small bowl, mix the drained tuna with the mayonnaise until well combined.
2. Add the chopped cucumber to the tuna mixture and mix well.
3. Season with salt and pepper to taste.
4. Spread the tuna mixture over the rice cake. Serve immediately.

Calories: 290
Carbs: 11g
Protein: 25g
Fat: 15g

BREAKFAST BURRITO WITH SCRAMBLED EGGS, PEPPERS, AND BACON

SERVINGS: 2
PREPARATION TIME: 20 minutes
INGREDIENTS
- 4 gluten-free tortillas
- 4 large eggs
- 2 strips of bacon, diced
- 1/2 red bell pepper, sliced

- 1/2 green bell pepper, sliced
- 2 tablespoons garlic-infused oil
- Salt and pepper to taste

INSTRUCTIONS

1. In a large skillet, cook the diced bacon over medium-high heat until crispy. Remove from the skillet and set aside on a paper towel to drain excess grease.
2. In the same skillet, add the sliced bell peppers and cook over medium-high heat until tender-crisp. Remove from the skillet and set aside.
3. Crack the eggs into a bowl and whisk until well beaten.
4. Heat the garlic-infused oil in the skillet over medium heat. Add the eggs to the skillet and cook, stirring occasionally, until scrambled and cooked through.
5. Warm the gluten-free tortillas in the microwave or on a skillet until soft and pliable.
6. To assemble the burritos, divide the scrambled eggs, bacon, and bell peppers among the tortillas. Roll up the tortillas tightly.

Calories: 462
Carbohydrates: 41g
Protein: 16g
Fat: 27g

CHIA SEED PUDDING WITH LOW FODMAP FRUITS AND COCONUT MILK

SERVINGS: 2
PREPARATION TIME: 10 minutes + overnight chilling

INGREDIENTS

- 1/4 cup chia seeds
- 1 cup low FODMAP coconut milk
- 1 tablespoon maple syrup
- 1/2 teaspoon vanilla extract
- 1/2 cup low FODMAP fruits (such as strawberries, blueberries, or raspberries)

INSTRUCTIONS

1. In a medium bowl, whisk together the chia seeds, coconut milk, maple syrup, and vanilla extract until well combined.
2. Stir in the low FODMAP fruits.
3. Cover the bowl with plastic wrap and refrigerate overnight or for at least 4 hours to allow the chia seeds to thicken and absorb the liquid.
4. Once the chia seed pudding has chilled and thickened, stir it well to break up any clumps and distribute the fruit evenly.
5. Divide the pudding between two serving dishes and top with additional low FODMAP fruits, if desired.

Calories: 250
Carbohydrates: 19g
Protein: 5g
Fat: 18g

GLUTEN-FREE GRANOLA WITH YOGURT AND LOW FODMAP FRUITS

SERVINGS: 2
PREPARATION TIME: 15 minutes

INGREDIENTS

- 1/2 cup gluten-free rolled oats
- 1/4 cup unsweetened shredded coconut
- 2 tablespoons chopped pecans
- 1 tablespoon maple syrup
- 1 tablespoon coconut oil
- 1/4 teaspoon ground cinnamon
- Pinch of salt
- 1 cup lactose-free yogurt
- 1/2 cup low FODMAP fruits (e.g., strawberries, blueberries, raspberries)

INSTRUCTIONS

1. Preheat the oven to 325°F (160°C).
2. In a mixing bowl, combine the gluten-free rolled oats, unsweetened shredded coconut, chopped pecans, maple syrup, coconut oil, ground cinnamon, and a pinch of salt.
3. Mix everything together until the oats are coated with the maple syrup and coconut oil.
4. Spread the mixture onto a baking sheet lined with parchment paper.
5. Bake for 10-12 minutes or until the granola is golden brown, stirring occasionally to prevent burning.
6. Remove the baking sheet from the oven and let the granola cool completely.
7. To assemble the breakfast bowls, divide the lactose-free yogurt between two bowls.
8. Top each bowl with the low FODMAP fruits and the cooled granola.
9. Serve and enjoy!

Calories: 350
Carbohydrates: 32g
Protein: 15g
Fat: 20g

BREAKFAST HASH WITH SWEET POTATOES, PEPPERS, AND SAUSAGE

SERVINGS: 4
PREPARATION TIME: 30 minutes

INGREDIENTS

- 2 large sweet potatoes, peeled and diced into 1/2 inch cubes
- 2 tablespoons olive oil
- 1/2 teaspoon paprika
- 1/2 teaspoon garlic powder
- Salt and pepper to taste
- 1 red bell pepper, diced
- 1 green bell pepper, diced
- 1 yellow onion, diced
- 4 gluten-free sausages, sliced into rounds
- 4 eggs

INSTRUCTIONS

1. Preheat the oven to 425°F.
2. Toss the sweet potato cubes with the olive oil, paprika, garlic powder, salt, and pepper in a large bowl until evenly coated.

3. Spread the seasoned sweet potatoes out in a single layer on a baking sheet.
4. Roast the sweet potatoes in the preheated oven for 20-25 minutes or until tender and lightly browned.
5. While the sweet potatoes are roasting, heat a large skillet over medium-high heat.
6. Add the diced bell peppers and onion to the skillet and sauté for 5-7 minutes or until softened.
7. Add the sliced sausage to the skillet and sauté for an additional 3-4 minutes or until lightly browned.
8. Divide the roasted sweet potatoes among four plates.
9. Top each plate with the sausage and pepper mixture.
10. Fry the eggs to your liking and place one egg on top of each plate.
11. Serve immediately.

Calories: 440
Carbs: 33g
Protein: 19g
Fat: 27g

GLUTEN-FREE PANCAKES WITH BLUEBERRIES AND MAPLE SYRUP

SERVINGS: 4
PREPARATION TIME: 20 minutes

INGREDIENTS
- 1 cup gluten-free all-purpose flour
- 2 tablespoons sugar
- 2 teaspoons baking powder
- 1/4 teaspoon salt
- 1 cup almond milk
- 2 tablespoons vegetable oil
- 1 large egg
- 1/2 cup fresh blueberries
- Maple syrup for serving

INSTRUCTIONS
1. In a large bowl, whisk together the gluten-free flour, sugar, baking powder, and salt.
2. In a separate bowl, whisk together the almond milk, vegetable oil, and egg.
3. Pour the wet **INGREDIENTS** into the dry **INGREDIENTS** and stir until just combined.
4. Fold in the blueberries.
5. Heat a non-stick skillet or griddle over medium-high heat.
6. Scoop 1/4 cup of the pancake batter onto the skillet for each pancake.
7. Cook for 2-3 minutes on each side or until golden brown.
8. Repeat with the remaining batter, adding more oil to the skillet as needed.
9. Serve the pancakes with maple syrup.

Calories: 267
Carbohydrates: 38g
Protein: 4g
Fat: 11g

SHAKSHUKA WITH TOMATO, BELL PEPPER, AND EGGS

SERVINGS: 4
PREPARATION TIME: 10 minutes
COOKING TIME 25 minutes

INGREDIENTS
- 2 tablespoons olive oil
- 1 red bell pepper, diced
- 1 yellow onion, diced
- 3 garlic cloves, minced
- 1 teaspoon smoked paprika
- 1/2 teaspoon ground cumin
- 1/4 teaspoon red pepper flakes
- 1 (28-ounce) can whole peeled tomatoes, crushed by hand
- 4-8 eggs
- Chopped fresh parsley or cilantro, for garnish

INSTRUCTIONS
1. Heat the olive oil in a large skillet over medium-high heat.
2. Add the diced bell pepper and onion and cook until softened, about 5-7 minutes.
3. Add the minced garlic, smoked paprika, ground cumin, and red pepper flakes, and cook for another 1-2 minutes until fragrant.
4. Add the crushed tomatoes and season with salt and black pepper to taste.
5. Simmer the tomato sauce over medium-low heat for 10-15 minutes, until it has thickened slightly.
6. Using a spoon, create small wells in the tomato sauce and crack an egg into each well.
7. Cover the skillet and let the eggs cook for 8-10 minutes, until the whites are set and the yolks are still runny.
8. Garnish with chopped fresh parsley or cilantro and serve hot.

Calories: 183
Carbohydrates: 12g
Protein: 9g
Fat: 12g

CHIA SEED PUDDING WITH LOW FODMAP FRUITS AND COCONUT MILK

SERVINGS: 2
PREPARATION TIME: 10 minutes

INGREDIENTS
- 1/4 cup chia seeds
- 1 cup unsweetened coconut milk
- 1 tablespoon maple syrup
- 1/4 teaspoon vanilla extract
- 1/2 cup low FODMAP fruits (e.g. strawberries, blueberries, kiwi, banana)
- 2 tablespoons unsweetened shredded coconut

INSTRUCTIONS

1. In a small bowl, whisk together the chia seeds, coconut milk, maple syrup, and vanilla extract.
2. Let the mixture sit for at least 5 minutes to thicken up, stirring occasionally.
3. In the meantime, slice the low FODMAP fruits.
4. Once the chia seed mixture has thickened to a pudding-like consistency, divide it between two small bowls.
5. Top each bowl with sliced low FODMAP fruits and unsweetened shredded coconut.
6. Serve immediately or chill in the refrigerator for later.
7. Calories: and Macro (Carbs:, Prot, Fat:)
8. Per serving

Calories: 212
Carbs: 20g
Protein: 4g
Fat: 14g

GLUTEN-FREE WAFFLES WITH STRAWBERRIES AND CREAM

SERVINGS: 4
PREPARATION TIME: 20 minutes

INGREDIENTS

- 1+1/2 cups gluten-free all-purpose flour
- 1 tablespoon baking powder
- 1/4 teaspoon salt and 1 tablespoon sugar
- 2 eggs, separated
- 1+1/2 cups almond milk
- 1/4 cup vegetable oil
- 1 teaspoon vanilla extract
- 1 cup fresh strawberries, sliced
- 1/2 cup whipped cream

INSTRUCTIONS

1. In a large bowl, whisk together the gluten-free flour, baking powder, salt, and sugar.
2. In a separate bowl, beat the egg whites until stiff peaks form.
3. In a small bowl, whisk together the egg yolks, almond milk, vegetable oil, and vanilla extract.
4. Add the wet ingredients to the dry ingredients and stir until well combined.
5. Gently fold in the beaten egg whites until just incorporated.
6. Preheat a waffle iron and spray with cooking spray.
7. Pour the batter into the waffle iron and cook according to the manufacturer's.
8. Serve the waffles topped with sliced strawberries and whipped cream.

Calories: 370
Carbohydrates: 36g
Protein: 8g
Fat: 23g

QUINOA BREAKFAST BOWL WITH SCRAMBLED EGGS AND AVOCADO

SERVINGS: 1
PREPARATION TIME: 15 minutes

INGREDIENTS

- 1/2 cup cooked quinoa
- 2 large eggs
- 1/4 avocado, sliced
- 1/4 cup diced red bell pepper
- 1/4 cup diced zucchini
- 1/4 cup chopped spinach
- 1/4 tsp. salt
- 1/4 tsp. black pepper
- 1 tbsp. olive oil

INSTRUCTIONS

1. In a medium skillet, heat olive oil over medium heat.
2. Add the red bell pepper, zucchini, and spinach to the skillet and sauté for 2-3 minutes, until the vegetables are tender.
3. Add the cooked quinoa to the skillet and stir well to combine with the vegetables. Season with salt and black pepper.
4. In a separate bowl, beat the eggs with a fork.
5. Pour the eggs into the skillet with the quinoa and vegetables, stirring constantly until the eggs are cooked through.
6. Transfer the quinoa and egg mixture to a bowl and top with sliced avocado.
7. Serve hot and enjoy!

Calories: 442
Carbs: 34g
Protein: 20g
Fat: 25g

AVOCADO AND QUINOA BREAKFAST BOWL

SERVINGS: 1
PREPARATION TIME: 20 minutes

INGREDIENTS

- 1/2 cup quinoa, rinsed
- 1 cup water
- 1/2 avocado, sliced
- 1 small tomato, chopped
- 1 scallion, sliced
- 1/4 cup canned black beans, drained and rinsed
- 1/4 teaspoon ground cumin
- 1/4 teaspoon smoked paprika
- Salt and pepper to taste
- 1 tablespoon olive oil
- 1 egg
- 1 teaspoon white vinegar
- 1/4 cup fresh spinach leaves

INSTRUCTIONS

1. In a medium saucepan, combine the quinoa and water. Bring to a boil, then reduce heat to low and cover. Cook for 15 minutes or until the water is absorbed and the quinoa is tender.
2. In a small bowl, combine the avocado, tomato, and scallion. Set aside.

3. In a small skillet, heat the black beans with the cumin, smoked paprika, and a pinch of salt and pepper. Cook for 2-3 minutes, stirring occasionally.
4. In another small skillet, heat the olive oil over medium heat. Crack the egg into the skillet and fry until the white is set but the yolk is still runny.
5. While the egg is cooking, bring a small pot of water to a boil. Add the white vinegar and stir. Reduce the heat to low and gently crack the egg into the water. Cook for 2-3 minutes or until the white is set but the yolk is still runny.
6. To assemble the breakfast bowl, start with a bed of fresh spinach leaves. Top with the cooked quinoa, black beans, and avocado mixture. Place the fried egg on top of the avocado mixture, and then add the poached egg on top of the fried egg.
7. Season with salt and pepper to taste.

Calories: 476
Carbs: 43g
Protein: 16g
Fat: 29g

BREAKFAST SANDWICH WITH GLUTEN-FREE BREAD, EGG, AND BACON

SERVINGS: 1
PREPARATION TIME: 10 minutes

INGREDIENTS

- 2 slices gluten-free bread
- 2 slices of bacon
- 1 egg
- Salt and pepper to taste
- 1 tablespoon of butter
- Optional lettuce, tomato, avocado

INSTRUCTIONS

1. Cook the bacon in a non-stick pan until crispy. Remove from pan and set aside.
2. In the same pan, melt the butter over medium heat.
3. Crack the egg into the pan and cook until the whites are set but the yolk is still runny, about 2-3 minutes. Sprinkle with salt and pepper.
4. Toast the gluten-free bread.
5. Assemble the sandwich by placing the cooked egg and bacon between the slices of toast. Add lettuce, tomato, and avocado if desired.
6. Serve immediately.

Calories: 435
Carbs: 36g
Protein: 22g
Fat: 23g

GLUTEN-FREE OATMEAL WITH RASPBERRIES AND ALMONDS

SERVINGS: 1
PREPARATION TIME: 10 minutes

INGREDIENTS
- 1/2 cup gluten-free oats
- 1 cup almond milk
- 1/4 cup fresh raspberries
- 1 tbsp sliced almonds
- 1 tbsp maple syrup

INSTRUCTIONS
1. In a small saucepan, bring almond milk to a simmer over medium heat.
2. Add gluten-free oats and stir to combine.
3. Cook for 5-7 minutes or until the oatmeal has thickened, stirring occasionally.
4. Remove from heat and let cool for a minute.
5. Top with fresh raspberries, sliced almonds, and a drizzle of maple syrup.

Calories: 305
Carbs: 49g
Protein: 9g
Fat: 8g

SCRAMBLED EGGS WITH SPINACH AND TOMATO

SERVINGS: 2
PREPARATION TIME: 15 minutes

INGREDIENTS
- 4 large eggs
- 1 cup fresh spinach, chopped
- 1 tomato, diced
- 1 tablespoon olive oil
- Salt and pepper to taste

INSTRUCTIONS
1. In a bowl, beat the eggs and season with salt and pepper.
2. Heat olive oil in a non-stick skillet over medium heat.
3. Add chopped spinach and diced tomato and cook for 2 minutes until wilted.
4. Pour beaten eggs into the skillet and cook, stirring, until eggs are set.
5. Serve hot.

Calories: 210
Carbs: 5g
Protein: 13g
Fat: 15g

BANANA AND BLUEBERRY SMOOTHIE

SERVINGS: 1
PREPARATION TIME: 5 minutes

INGREDIENTS
- 1 ripe banana
- 1/2 cup blueberries
- 1 cup lactose-free yogurt
- 1 tablespoon honey
- Ice cubes (optional)

INSTRUCTIONS
1. Combine banana, blueberries, lactose-free yogurt, and honey in a blender.
2. Blend until smooth.
3. Add ice cubes if desired and blend again.
4. Pour into a glass and enjoy.

Calories: 290
Carbs: 62g
Protein: 5g
Fat: 3g

PEANUT BUTTER AND BANANA RICE CAKES

SERVINGS: 2
PREPARATION TIME: 5 minutes

INGREDIENTS
- 2 rice cakes (check for low-FODMAP)
- 2 tablespoons peanut butter (without added high-FODMAP **INGREDIENTS**)
- 1 ripe banana, sliced

INSTRUCTIONS
1. Spread peanut butter evenly on the rice cakes.
2. Top with banana slices and serve as a quick

Calories: 220
Carbs: 33g
Protein: 5g
Fat: 9g

OMELETTE WITH SPINACH AND FETA

SERVINGS: 2
PREPARATION TIME: 15 minutes

INGREDIENTS
- 4 large eggs
- 1 cup fresh spinach, chopped
- 1/4 cup lactose-free feta cheese, crumbled
- 1 tablespoon olive oil
- Salt and pepper to taste

INSTRUCTIONS
1. In a bowl, beat the eggs and season with salt and pepper.
2. Heat olive oil in a non-stick skillet over medium heat.
3. Add chopped spinach and cook for 2 minutes until wilted.
4. Pour beaten eggs into the skillet and cook until set.
5. Sprinkle crumbled feta cheese on one half of the omelette, then fold the other half over it.
6. Serve hot.

Calories: 260
Carbs: 2g
Protein: 15g
Fat: 20g

QUINOA BREAKFAST BOWL

SERVINGS: 2
PREPARATION TIME: 20 minutes

INGREDIENTS
- 1 cup cooked quinoa
- 1/2 cup lactose-free yogurt
- 1/2 cup strawberries, sliced
- 2 tablespoons maple syrup (use pure maple syrup)
- 2 tablespoons chopped nuts (e.g., almonds or walnuts)
- 1/2 teaspoon cinnamon

INSTRUCTIONS
1. Divide cooked quinoa into two bowls.
2. Top each bowl with lactose-free yogurt, sliced strawberries, maple syrup, chopped nuts, and a sprinkle of cinnamon.
3. Mix together before eating.

Calories: 320
Carbs: 50g
Protein: 9g
Fat: 10g

BLUEBERRY PANCAKES

SERVINGS: 2
PREPARATION TIME: 25 minutes

INGREDIENTS
- 1 cup gluten-free pancake mix (check for low-FODMAP)
- 1/2 cup lactose-free milk
- 1/2 cup blueberries
- 1 tablespoon vegetable oil
- Maple syrup (use pure maple syrup) for drizzling

INSTRUCTIONS
1. In a mixing bowl, combine pancake mix and lactose-free milk until well blended.
2. Gently fold in blueberries.
3. Heat a non-stick skillet over medium heat and add vegetable oil.
4. Pour 1/4 cup of pancake batter onto the skillet for each pancake.
5. Cook until bubbles form on the surface, then flip and cook until golden brown.
6. Serve with a drizzle of maple syrup.

Calories: 330
Carbs: 50g
Protein: 6g
Fat: 11g

CHIA SEED PUDDING

SERVINGS: 2
PREPARATION TIME: 5 minutes
(plus chilling time)

INGREDIENTS
- 1/4 cup chia seeds
- 1 cup lactose-free milk
- 1 tablespoon maple syrup (use pure maple syrup)
- 1/2 teaspoon vanilla extract
- Fresh berries for topping

INSTRUCTIONS
1. In a bowl, mix chia seeds, lactose-free milk, maple syrup, and vanilla extract.
2. Stir well and refrigerate for at least 4 hours or overnight until the mixture thickens.
3. Before serving, top with fresh berries.

Calories: 180
Carbs: 22g
Protein: 5g
Fat: 8g

GREEK YOGURT PARFAIT

SERVINGS: 2
PREPARATION TIME: 10 minutes

INGREDIENTS
- 2 cups lactose-free Greek yogurt
- 1/2 cup granola (check for low-FODMAP)
- 1/2 cup strawberries, sliced
- 2 tablespoons honey
- Fresh mint leaves for garnish

INSTRUCTIONS
1. In two glasses or bowls, layer lactose-free Greek yogurt, granola, and sliced strawberries.
2. Drizzle honey over the top and garnish with fresh mint leaves.
3. Serve chilled.

Calories: 290
Carbs: 40g
Protein: 13g
Fat: 9g

RICE CAKE WITH SMOKED SALMON

SERVINGS: 2
PREPARATION TIME: 10 minutes

INGREDIENTS
- 2 rice cakes (check for low-FODMAP)
- 4 ounces smoked salmon
- 2 tablespoons lactose-free cream cheese
- Fresh dill for garnish
- Lemon wedges for serving

INSTRUCTIONS
1. Spread lactose-free cream cheese on the rice cakes.
2. Top each rice cake with smoked salmon and garnish with fresh dill.

3. Serve with lemon wedges for squeezing over the salmon.

Calories: 210
Carbs: 8g
Protein: 14g
Fat: 13g

VEGGIE AND BACON FRITTATA

SERVINGS: 4
PREPARATION TIME: 30 minutes

INGREDIENTS
- 6 large eggs
- 1/2 cup lactose-free milk
- 4 slices bacon, cooked and crumbled
- 1 cup zucchini, diced
- 1 cup red bell pepper, diced
- 1/2 cup scallions (green parts only), chopped
- Salt and pepper to taste

INSTRUCTIONS
1. Preheat oven to 350°F (175°C).
2. In a bowl, whisk together eggs, lactose-free milk, crumbled bacon, salt, and pepper.
3. In an oven-safe skillet, sauté diced zucchini, diced red bell pepper, and chopped scallions over medium heat until tender.
4. Pour the egg mixture over the sautéed vegetables.
5. Bake in the oven for 15-20 minutes until the frittata is set.
6. Slice and serve.
7. Enjoy!

Calories: 250
Carbs: 4g
Protein: 15g
Fat: 19g

PEANUT BUTTER BANANA SMOOTHIE BOWL

SERVINGS: 1
PREPARATION TIME: 10 minutes

INGREDIENTS
- 1 ripe banana
- 2 tablespoons peanut butter (without high-FODMAP **INGREDIENTS**)
- 1/2 cup lactose-free yogurt
- 1/4 cup oats
- 1 tablespoon chia seeds
- Sliced strawberries and blueberries for topping

INSTRUCTIONS
1. In a blender, combine banana, peanut butter, lactose-free yogurt, oats, and chia seeds.
2. Blend until smooth.
3. Pour the mixture into a bowl.
4. Top with sliced strawberries and blueberries.
5. Enjoy with a spoon!

Calories: 430
Carbs: 55g
Protein: 12g
Fat: 20g

VEGGIE BREAKFAST BURRITO

SERVINGS: 2
PREPARATION TIME: 20 minutes

INGREDIENTS
- 4 large eggs
- 1/2 cup red bell pepper, diced
- 1/2 cup zucchini, diced
- 2 tablespoons olive oil
- Salt and pepper to taste
- 2 gluten-free tortillas (check for low-FODMAP)

INSTRUCTIONS
1. In a skillet, heat olive oil over medium heat.
2. Add diced red bell pepper and zucchini and sauté until tender.
3. In a separate bowl, beat the eggs, then pour them into the skillet with the sautéed veggies.
4. Cook, stirring occasionally, until the eggs are set.
5. Season with salt and pepper.
6. Warm the tortillas in a dry skillet or microwave.
7. Divide the egg mixture between the tortillas, roll them up, and serve.

Calories: 310
Carbs: 20g
Protein: 14g
Fat: 20g

RASPBERRY CHIA SEED PUDDING

SERVINGS: 2
PREPARATION TIME: 5 minutes (plus chilling time)

INGREDIENTS
- 1/4 cup chia seeds
- 1 cup lactose-free milk
- 1/2 cup raspberries
- 1 tablespoon maple syrup (use pure maple syrup)

INSTRUCTIONS
1. In a bowl, mix chia seeds, lactose-free milk, maple syrup, and raspberries.
2. Stir well and refrigerate for at least 4 hours or overnight until the mixture thickens.
3. Serve topped with additional raspberries if desired.

Calories: 190
Carbs: 22g
Protein: 5g
Fat: 9g

SPINACH AND FETA WRAP

SERVINGS: 2
PREPARATION TIME: 15 minutes

INGREDIENTS
- 4 large eggs
- 1 cup fresh spinach, chopped
- 1/4 cup lactose-free feta cheese, crumbled
- 2 gluten-free tortillas (check for low-FODMAP)
- Salt and pepper to taste

INSTRUCTIONS
1. In a bowl, beat the eggs and season with salt and pepper.
2. Heat a non-stick skillet over medium heat.
3. Add chopped spinach and cook until wilted.
4. Pour beaten eggs into the skillet and cook until set.
5. Sprinkle crumbled lactose-free feta cheese over one half of each tortilla, then fold the other half over it.
6. Divide the scrambled eggs mixture between the two tortillas. Roll them up and serve.

Calories: 300
Carbs: 20g
Protein: 15g
Fat: 18g

LOW-FODMAP PANCAKES

SERVINGS: 2
PREPARATION TIME: 20 minutes

INGREDIENTS
- 1 cup gluten-free pancake mix (check for low-FODMAP)
- 1/2 cup lactose-free milk
- 1 tablespoon vegetable oil
- 1 tablespoon maple syrup (use pure maple syrup)
- 1/2 teaspoon vanilla extract

INSTRUCTIONS
1. In a mixing bowl, combine pancake mix, lactose-free milk, vegetable oil, maple syrup, and vanilla extract until well blended.
2. Heat a non-stick skillet over medium heat.
3. Pour 1/4 cup of pancake batter onto the skillet for each pancake.
4. Cook until bubbles form on the surface, then flip and cook until golden brown.
5. Serve with a drizzle of maple syrup.

Calories: 280
Carbs: 38g
Protein: 4g
Fat: 12g

BACON AND TOMATO OMELETTE

SERVINGS: 2
PREPARATION TIME: 15 minutes

INGREDIENTS
- 4 large eggs
- 2 slices bacon, cooked and crumbled
- 1 tomato, diced
- 1 tablespoon olive oil
- Salt and pepper to taste

INSTRUCTIONS
1. In a bowl, beat the eggs and season with salt and pepper.
2. Heat olive oil in a non-stick skillet over medium heat.
3. Add diced tomato and cook for 2 minutes.
4. Pour beaten eggs into the skillet and cook until set.
5. Sprinkle crumbled bacon over one half of the omelette, then fold the other half over it.
6. Serve hot.

Calories: 230
Carbs: 2g
Protein: 13g
Fat: 19g

STRAWBERRY AND ALMOND BUTTER TOAST

SERVINGS: 2
PREPARATION TIME: 5 minutes

INGREDIENTS
- 2 slices gluten-free bread (check for low-FODMAP)
- 4 tablespoons almond butter (without high-FODMAP **INGREDIENTS**)
- 1 cup strawberries, sliced

INSTRUCTIONS
1. Toast the gluten-free bread slices.
2. Spread 2 tablespoons of almond butter on each slice.
3. Top with sliced strawberries.
4. Serve as an open-faced sandwich.

Calories: 280
Carbs: 24g
Protein: 7g
Fat: 18g

BREAKFAST QUICHE WITH SPINACH AND BACON

SERVINGS: 4
PREPARATION TIME: 35 minutes

INGREDIENTS
- 6 large eggs
- 1/2 cup lactose-free milk
- 2 cups fresh spinach, chopped
- 4 slices bacon, cooked and crumbled
- Salt and pepper to taste

INSTRUCTIONS
1. Preheat oven to 375°F (190°C).
2. In a bowl, whisk together eggs, lactose-free milk, salt, and pepper.
3. Stir in chopped spinach and crumbled bacon.
4. Pour the mixture into a greased pie dish.
5. Bake for 20-25 minutes until the quiche is set and the top is golden.
6. Slice and serve.

Calories: 240
Carbs: 2g
Protein: 16g
Fat: 18g

MIXED BERRY OVERNIGHT OATS

SERVINGS: 2
PREPARATION TIME: 5 minutes (plus chilling time)

INGREDIENTS
- 1 cup rolled oats (check for low-FODMAP)
- 2 cups lactose-free milk
- 1/2 cup mixed berries (e.g., blueberries, raspberries, strawberries)
- 2 tablespoons maple syrup (use pure maple syrup)
-

INSTRUCTIONS
1. In a bowl, combine rolled oats, lactose-free milk, mixed berries, and maple syrup.
2. Stir well and refrigerate overnight.
3. In the morning, give it a good stir before serving.

Calories: 310
Carbs: 54g
Protein: 10g
Fat: 6g

TOFU SCRAMBLE WITH SPINACH AND TOMATOES

SERVINGS: 2
PREPARATION TIME: 20 minutes

INGREDIENTS

- 8 ounces firm tofu, crumbled
- 1 cup fresh spinach, chopped
- 1 tomato, diced
- 1/2 teaspoon turmeric powder
- Salt and pepper to taste

INSTRUCTIONS

1. In a skillet, sauté crumbled tofu with chopped spinach, diced tomato, and turmeric powder over medium heat.
2. Cook until heated through and spinach wilts.
3. Season with salt and pepper.
4. Serve hot.

Calories: 140
Carbs: 6g
Protein: 12g
Fat: 8g

MEAT

GRILLED CHICKEN WITH ROASTED VEGETABLES

SERVINGS: 4
PREPARATION TIME: 30 minutes

INGREDIENTS

- 4 boneless, skinless chicken breasts
- 2 bell peppers, sliced
- 1 zucchini, sliced
- 1 eggplant, sliced
- 2 tbsp olive oil
- Salt and pepper to taste

INSTRUCTIONS

1. Prepare a grill with medium-high heat.
2. Rub salt and pepper onto both sides of the chicken breasts.
3. Season veggies with salt and pepper and brush with olive oil.
4. Fire up the grill, and cook the chicken for 6 to 8 minutes each side, or until it reaches an internal temperature of 165 degrees.
5. Roast the veggies at 400 degrees Fahrenheit for 15 to 20 minutes, or until soft, while the chicken is in the oven.
6. Prepare the roasted veggies and serve them beside the chicken.

Calories: 290
Carbs: 9g
Protein: 38g
Fat: 11g

TURKEY AND LETTUCE WRAP

SERVINGS: 2
PREPARATION TIME: 15 minutes

INGREDIENTS

- 4 large lettuce leaves
- 8 oz cooked turkey breast, sliced
- 1/2 red bell pepper, sliced
- 1/2 cucumber, sliced
- 1/2 avocado, sliced
- 2 tbsp low FODMAP mayonnaise
- 1 tbsp Dijon mustard
- Salt and pepper, to taste

INSTRUCTIONS

1. Spread the lettuce leaves out on a surface that has been well cleaned.
2. Mayonnaise and Dijon mustard should be combined in a low-volume container first.
3. On the lettuce leaves, spread the mayonnaise and mustard mixture that has been combined.
4. Sliced turkey, red bell pepper, cucumber, and avocado should be placed on top of each leaf of lettuce.
5. The desired amount of salt and pepper should be sprinkled on top.
6. Wrap each individual lettuce leaf like a wrap and then serve.

Calories: per serving 266
Carbohydrates: 7g
Protein: 33g
Fat: 12g

LOW FODMAP CHICKEN AND VEGETABLE SKEWERS

SERVINGS: 4
PREPARATION TIME: 30 minutes

INGREDIENTS
- 2 boneless, skinless chicken breasts, cut into 1-inch cubes
- 1 red bell pepper, seeded and cut into 1-inch pieces
- 1 zucchini, sliced into 1-inch rounds
- 1 tablespoon garlic-infused olive oil
- 1 tablespoon lemon juice
- 1 teaspoon dried oregano
- Salt and black pepper, to taste
- Wooden skewers

INSTRUCTIONS
1. Prepare the grill or grill pan by heating it to a medium-high temperature.
2. Olive oil that has been infused with garlic is combined with lemon juice, dried oregano, salt, and black pepper in a large bowl with a whisk.
3. After adding the chicken, bell pepper, and zucchini to the bowl, mix everything together so that the marinade evenly coats the veggies as well as the chicken.
4. Skewer the chicken and veggies on the wooden skewers in a manner that alternates between the two ingredients.
5. Cook the skewers over a grill for ten to twelve minutes, turning them every so often, until the chicken is completely cooked through and the veggies are soft but still have a charred flavor.
6. Warm the skewers and accompany them with a salad or rice on the side.

Calories: 170
Carbohydrates: 5g
Protein: 26g,
Fat: 5g

CHICKEN AND VEGETABLE KEBABS WITH QUINOA

SERVINGS: 4
PREPARATION TIME: 25 minutes

INGREDIENTS
- 1 lb boneless, skinless chicken breasts, cut into cubes
- 2 bell peppers, cut into chunks
- 1 zucchini, cut into chunks
- 1 yellow squash, cut into chunks
- 1/4 cup olive oil
- 1 tbsp. garlic-infused oil
- 1 tbsp. fresh lemon juice
- 1 tsp. dried oregano
- 1/2 tsp. salt
- 1/4 tsp. black pepper
- 1 cup cooked quinoa

INSTRUCTIONS

1. Prepare the grill for cooking over medium-high heat.
2. Mix together olive oil, oil that has been infused with garlic, lemon juice, oregano, salt, and black pepper in a small bowl using a whisk.
3. Skewers should be loaded with chicken, red and green bell peppers, zucchini, and yellow squash.
4. Coat the skewers with the olive oil and garlic mixture and set aside.
5. Cook the skewers over a grill for ten to twelve minutes, turning them every so often, until the chicken is completely cooked through and the veggies are soft.
6. Serve on quinoa that has been cooked.

Calories: 387
Carbohydrates: 25g
Protein: 27g
Fat: 19g

LOW FODMAP CHICKEN AND VEGETABLE STIR-FRY WITH RICE NOODLES

SERVINGS: 4
PREPARATION TIME: 20 min

INGREDIENTS

- 8 oz. low FODMAP rice noodles
- 2 tbsp. olive oil
- 1 lb. boneless, skinless chicken breast, cut into thin strips
- 1 red bell pepper, sliced
- 1 yellow bell pepper, sliced
- 1 zucchini, sliced
- 1 cup snow peas
- 2 tbsp. low FODMAP soy sauce
- 2 tbsp. oyster sauce
- 1 tsp. garlic-infused oil
- 1 tsp. grated fresh ginger
- Salt and pepper to taste
- Sesame seeds for garnish

INSTRUCTIONS

1. Rice noodles should be prepared in accordance with the instructions provided on the box. Drain, then put to the side.
2. Olive oil should be heated up over high heat in a wok or a big pan.
3. Stir-fry the chicken for three to four minutes, or until it is completely cooked through.
4. Stir fry the bell peppers, zucchini, and snow peas for two to three minutes, or until the veggies reach a crisp-tender consistency, whichever comes first.
5. In a pan over medium heat, combine cooked rice noodles, oyster sauce, soy sauce, oil infused with garlic, grated ginger, and a pinch each of salt and pepper. Cook for a further one to two minutes after giving everything a good toss.
6. To serve, bring to a boil and sprinkle with toasted sesame seeds.

Calories: 398
Carbohydrates: 52g
Protein: 28g
Fat: 9g

TURKEY AND POTATO HASH

SERVINGS: 4
PREPARATION TIME: 30 minutes

INGREDIENTS
- 1 pound ground turkey
- 4 cups diced potatoes
- 2 tablespoons olive oil
- 1 teaspoon dried thyme
- Salt and pepper to taste

INSTRUCTIONS
1. In a large skillet, heat olive oil over medium heat.
2. Add diced potatoes and cook until they start to brown, about 10 minutes.
3. Push potatoes to one side and add ground turkey to the skillet. Cook until browned.
4. Mix turkey and potatoes, then add dried thyme, salt, and pepper. Cook for an additional 5 minutes until potatoes are tender.

Calories: 280
Carbs: 22g
Protein: 20g
Fat: 13g

LOW FODMAP CHICKEN CAESAR SALAD

SERVINGS: 4
PREPARATION TIME: 15 minutes

INGREDIENTS
- 1 lb boneless, skinless chicken breasts
- 1 head of romaine lettuce, chopped
- 1/2 cup cherry tomatoes, halved
- 1/2 cup cucumber, sliced
- 1/4 cup grated Parmesan cheese
- 1/4 cup low FODMAP Caesar dressing
- Salt and pepper to taste

INSTRUCTIONS
1. Turn the oven up to 400 degrees Fahrenheit.
2. Add some salt and pepper to the chicken breasts, then place them in the oven for 20 to 25 minutes, or until the chicken is completely cooked.
3. While the chicken is in the oven, you may cut the lettuce and cucumber into thin slices and cut the cherry tomatoes in half.
4. Combine the Caesar dressing and the Parmesan cheese in a small bowl and whisk until smooth.
5. Wait five minutes after the chicken has finished cooking before slicing it once you have given it time to rest.
6. Combine the chopped lettuce, sliced cucumber, and half cherry tomatoes in a large bowl and toss to combine.

7. Place the cut chicken in the bowl, then pour the Caesar dressing mixture over the chicken. Serve immediately.
8. Mix everything together until the salad is completely covered in the dressing and the ingredients are uniformly distributed.
9. Serve, and have fun with it!

Calories: 200
Carbohydrates: 6g
Protein: 26g
Fat: 8g

LOW FODMAP CHICKEN AND VEGETABLE SKEWERS WITH QUINOA

SERVINGS: 4
PREPARATION TIME: 30 minutes

INGREDIENTS
For the skewers
- 1 lb boneless, skinless chicken breasts, cut into 1-inch pieces
- 2 red bell peppers, seeded and cut into 1-inch pieces
- 2 zucchinis, sliced into rounds
- 1 tablespoon garlic-infused olive oil
- 1/2 teaspoon dried oregano
- Salt and pepper, to taste
- Wooden skewers, soaked in water for 30 minutes
For the quinoa

- 1 cup quinoa, rinsed and drained
- 2 cups water
- 1/4 teaspoon salt
- For the dressing
- 1/4 cup freshly squeezed lemon juice
- 1/4 cup extra-virgin olive oil
- 1 tablespoon Dijon mustard
- 1 tablespoon honey
- Salt and pepper, to taste

INSTRUCTIONS
1. Prepare the grill by heating it to a medium-high temperature.
2. Mix the chicken, bell peppers, zucchini, garlic-infused olive oil, oregano, and salt and pepper together in a large bowl. Mix everything together until the chicken and veggies are uniformly covered.
3. Skewer the chicken and veggies, rotating between each one as you go, using the skewers.
4. Cook the kebabs on the grill for 12 to 15 minutes, flipping them every so often, until the chicken is completely cooked through and the veggies are soft.
5. Prepare the quinoa while the skewers are in the grilling process. The quinoa, water, and salt should be brought to a boil in a pot of medium size. Turn the heat down to low, cover the pot, and let it simmer for 15 to 20 minutes, or until the quinoa is cooked through and all of the water has been absorbed.
6. To prepare the dressing, take a small bowl and mix together the lemon juice, olive oil, Dijon

mustard, honey, and seasonings of your choice (salt and pepper).

7. The skewers should be served with quinoa, and the dressing should be brought on the side.

Calories: 350
Carbohydrates: 30g
Protein: 26g
Fat: 14g

TURKEY LETTUCE WRAPS WITH LOW FODMAP DIPPING SAUCE

SERVINGS: 4
PREPARATION TIME: 30 minutes

INGREDIENTS

- For the lettuce wraps
- 1 pound ground turkey
- 1 tablespoon olive oil
- 1 tablespoon garlic-infused oil
- 2 tablespoons low FODMAP soy sauce
- 1 teaspoon ground ginger
- 1 teaspoon rice vinegar
- 1/4 teaspoon black pepper
- 1/4 teaspoon salt
- 8 large lettuce leaves, such as Bibb or butter lettuce
- 1/4 cup shredded carrots
- 1/4 cup chopped scallions (green parts only)
- 1/4 cup chopped cilantro
- 1/4 cup chopped peanuts
- For the low FODMAP dipping sauce

- 2 tablespoons low FODMAP soy sauce
- 2 tablespoons rice vinegar
- 1 tablespoon maple syrup
- 1 tablespoon garlic-infused oil
- 1/4 teaspoon ground ginger
- 1/4 teaspoon red pepper flakes

INSTRUCTIONS

1. Warm the olive oil and the oil that has been infused with garlic in a large pan over medium heat. After adding the ground turkey, sauté it over medium heat until it is browned, breaking it up with a wooden spoon as it cooks.

2. Combine the low FODMAP soy sauce, the ground ginger, the rice vinegar, the black pepper, and the salt in a small bowl and whisk to combine. After pouring the sauce over the turkey that has been cooked, toss it to blend the ingredients. Continue to cook for an additional two to three minutes.

3. In order to produce the dipping sauce that is low in FODMAPs, combine in a small bowl the soy sauce that is low in FODMAPs, the rice vinegar, the maple syrup, the garlic-infused oil, the ground ginger, and the red pepper flakes.

4. To make the lettuce wraps, just place a little of the turkey mixture on each leaf of lettuce using a spoon. Garnish with shredded carrots, sliced scallions and peanuts, chopped cilantro, and fresh cilantro. To accompany the dish, low FODMAP dipping sauce should be served on the side.

Per serving
Calories: 247
Carbs: 6g
Protein: 23g
Fat: 15g

TURKEY AND SPINACH STUFFED BELL PEPPERS

SERVINGS: 4
PREPARATION TIME: 50 minutes

INGREDIENTS
- 4 bell peppers, tops removed and seeds removed
- 1 pound ground turkey
- 2 cups fresh spinach, chopped
- 1 cup cooked quinoa
- 1 cup canned diced tomatoes (without onion or garlic)
- Salt and pepper to taste

INSTRUCTIONS
1. Preheat oven to 375°F (190°C).
2. In a skillet, cook ground turkey over medium heat until browned.
3. Stir in chopped spinach and cook until wilted.
4. In a bowl, mix cooked quinoa, cooked turkey mixture, diced tomatoes, salt, and pepper.
5. Stuff each bell pepper with the mixture and bake for 30 min.

Calories: 320
Carbs: 32g
Protein: 24g
Fat: 10g

ROASTED LEMON HERB CHICKEN THIGHS

SERVINGS: 4
PREPARATION TIME: 35 minutes

INGREDIENTS
- 4 bone-in, skin-on chicken thighs
- 2 tablespoons olive oil
- 1 lemon (juice and zest)
- 2 teaspoons dried rosemary
- Salt and pepper to taste

INSTRUCTIONS
1. Preheat oven to 375°F (190°C).
2. In a bowl, combine olive oil, lemon juice, lemon zest, dried rosemary, salt, and pepper.
3. Rub the mixture over the chicken thighs.
4. Place chicken on a baking sheet and roast for 25-30 minutes until cooked through.

Calories: 320
Carbs: 2g
Protein: 22g
Fat: 25g

PORK TENDERLOIN WITH MAPLE GLAZE

SERVINGS: 4
PREPARATION TIME: 35 minutes

INGREDIENTS
- 1 pound pork tenderloin
- 2 tablespoons maple syrup (use pure maple syrup)
- 1 tablespoon Dijon mustard
- 1 teaspoon fresh rosemary, minced
- Salt and pepper to taste

INSTRUCTIONS
1. Preheat oven to 375°F (190°C).
2. In a bowl, mix maple syrup, Dijon mustard, fresh rosemary, salt, and pepper.
3. Brush the mixture over the pork tenderloin.
4. Roast for 25-30 minutes until the pork reaches an internal temperature of 145°F (63°C).
5. Allow the meat to rest for a few minutes before slicing.

Calories: 230
Carbs: 9g
Protein: 24g
Fat: 9g

TURKEY AND CRANBERRY STUFFED ACORN SQUASH

SERVINGS: 2
PREPARATION TIME: 50 minutes

INGREDIENTS
- 2 acorn squash, halved and seeds removed
- 1 cup cooked ground turkey
- 1/2 cup cranberry sauce (made with glucose syrup)
- 1/4 cup fresh parsley, chopped
- Salt and pepper to taste

INSTRUCTIONS
1. Preheat oven to 375°F (190°C).
2. Place acorn squash halves, cut side down, on a baking sheet and roast for 30-35 minutes until tender.
3. In a bowl, combine cooked ground turkey, cranberry sauce, fresh parsley, salt, and pepper.
4. Fill each acorn squash half with the turkey mixture.
5. Bake for an additional 10-15 minutes to heat through.

Calories: 340
Carbs: 56g
Protein: 20g
Fat: 6g

GREEK SALAD WITH GRILLED CHICKEN

SERVINGS: 4
PREPARATION TIME: 30 minutes

INGREDIENTS

- 2 boneless, skinless chicken breasts
- 2 cups mixed salad greens
- 1 cucumber, diced
- 1 cup cherry tomatoes, halved
- 1/4 cup kalamata olives
- 1/4 cup crumbled feta cheese (lactose-free)
- 2 tablespoons olive oil
- 1 tablespoon fresh oregano, chopped
- Salt and pepper to taste

INSTRUCTIONS

1. Preheat grill to medium-high heat.
2. Season chicken breasts with olive oil, fresh oregano, salt, and pepper.
3. Grill chicken for 6-8 minutes per side until cooked through.
4. In a large bowl, combine mixed salad greens, diced cucumber, cherry tomatoes, kalamata olives, and crumbled feta cheese.
5. 5lice grilled chicken and place on top of the salad.
6. Serve with your favorite low-FODMAP dressing.
7. Enjoy!

Calories: 330
Carbs: 9g
Protein: 28g
Fat: 20g

GRILLED CHICKEN WITH LOW FODMAP VEGETABLES AND BROWN RICE

SERVINGS: 4
PREPARATION TIME: 10 minutes

INGREDIENTS

- 4 boneless, skinless chicken breasts
- 1 cup low FODMAP vegetables, such as bell peppers, zucchini, and eggplant, sliced
- 1 tbsp. garlic-infused oil
- 2 tbsp. low FODMAP balsamic vinaigrette
- 2 cups cooked brown rice
- Salt and pepper to taste

INSTRUCTIONS

1. Prepare the grill by heating it to a medium-high temperature.
2. Add salt and pepper to the chicken breasts before cooking them.
3. Toss the veggies in a big bowl with some garlic-infused oil, and then season them with salt and pepper to taste.
4. Cook the chicken on the grill for 6–8 minutes each side, or until it is fully done.
5. Grill the veggies for 3-4 minutes each side or until tender.
6. Blend the balsamic vinaigrette **INGREDIENTS** together in a small bowl using a whisk.
7. Brown rice that has been cooked should be served as the base for the chicken and veggies that have been grilled, and the

balsamic vinaigrette should be drizzled on top.

Calories: per serving 356
Carbohydrates: 39g
Protein: 32g
Fat: 8g

CHICKEN AND VEGETABLE STIR-FRY

SERVINGS: 4
PREPARATION TIME: 30 minutes

INGREDIENTS

- 1 pound boneless, skinless chicken breasts, sliced
- 2 cups broccoli florets
- 1 red bell pepper, sliced
- 2 carrots, sliced
- 2 tablespoons sesame oil
- 2 tablespoons low-sodium soy sauce (check for FODMAP-friendly version)
- 1 tablespoon fresh ginger, minced
- Salt and pepper to taste

INSTRUCTIONS

1. In a large skillet or wok, heat sesame oil over medium-high heat.
2. Add chicken slices and cook until browned and cooked through.
3. Add broccoli, red bell pepper, carrots, and fresh ginger. Stir-fry for 5-7 minutes until vegetables are tender.

4. Stir in soy sauce, salt, and pepper.
5. Serve hot.

Calories: 280
Carbs: 10g
Protein: 30g
Fat: 13g

CHICKEN AND VEGETABLE KABOBS WITH BROWN RICE

SERVINGS: 4
PREPARATION TIME: 30 minutes

INGREDIENTS

- 2 chicken breasts, cut into 1-inch cubes
- 1 red bell pepper, cut into 1-inch pieces
- 1 yellow bell pepper, cut into 1-inch pieces
- 1 zucchini, cut into 1/2-inch rounds
- 1/4 cup olive oil
- 1/4 cup low-sodium soy sauce
- 2 tablespoons honey
- 2 tablespoons minced fresh ginger
- 1 tablespoon minced garlic
- 1 tablespoon sesame oil
- Salt and pepper, to taste
- 2 cups cooked brown rice

INSTRUCTIONS

1. Preheat grill to medium-high heat.
2. In a large bowl, whisk together olive oil, soy sauce, honey, ginger, garlic, sesame oil, salt, and pepper. Reserve 1/4 cup of the mixture for basting later.
3. Add chicken, bell peppers, and zucchini to the bowl with the marinade. Toss to coat and let sit for 10-15 minutes.
4. Thread the chicken and vegetables onto skewers, alternating between the chicken and veggies.
5. Grill the skewers for 8-10 minutes per side, basting with the reserved marinade every few minutes.
6. Serve the kabobs with brown rice.

Calories: 360
Carbs: 45g
Protein: 28g
Fat: 9g

LOW FODMAP CHICKEN AND VEGETABLE STIR-FRY WITH QUINOA

SERVINGS: 4
PREPARATION TIME: 30 minutes

INGREDIENTS

- 1 cup quinoa
- 2 cups water
- 2 tablespoons olive oil
- 2 boneless, skinless chicken breasts, sliced into strips
- 1 red bell pepper, sliced
- 1 yellow bell pepper, sliced
- 1 small zucchini, sliced
- 2 tablespoons low FODMAP soy sauce
- 1 tablespoon grated fresh ginger
- 2 tablespoons chopped green onion (green part only)
- Salt and pepper, to taste

INSTRUCTIONS

1. Rinse the quinoa in a fine mesh strainer and place it in a pot with 2 cups of water. Bring to a boil, reduce heat, and simmer for 15-20 minutes, until the water is absorbed and the quinoa is tender. Fluff with a fork and set aside.
2. Heat 1 tablespoon of olive oil in a large skillet over medium-high heat. Add the chicken and cook for 5-7 minutes, until browned and cooked through. Remove the chicken from the skillet and set aside.
3. Add the remaining tablespoon of olive oil to the skillet. Add the bell peppers and zucchini and cook for 5-7 minutes, until the vegetables are tender-crisp.
4. Return the chicken to the skillet with the vegetables. Add the low FODMAP soy sauce, grated ginger, and chopped green onion. Stir to combine and cook for 2-3 minutes, until everything is heated through.
5. Divide the quinoa among four plates and top each with a portion of the chicken and

vegetable stir-fry. Season with salt and pepper, if desired.

Calories: 326
Carbs: 35g
Protein: 26g
Fat: 9g

GRILLED PORK TENDERLOIN WITH ROASTED CARROTS AND PARSNIPS

SERVINGS: 4
PREPARATION TIME: 1 hour

INGREDIENTS
- 1 pound pork tenderloin
- 1 teaspoon garlic powder
- 1 teaspoon onion powder
- 1 teaspoon smoked paprika
- 1/2 teaspoon salt
- 1/4 teaspoon black pepper
- 1 tablespoon olive oil
- 1 pound carrots, peeled and sliced into sticks
- 1 pound parsnips, peeled and sliced into sticks
- 2 tablespoons olive oil
- Salt and pepper to taste

INSTRUCTIONS
1. Lightly oil the grill grates and set the grill to medium-high heat.
2. Garlic powder, onion powder, smoked paprika, salt, and black pepper should be combined in a small bowl.
3. Use the spice blend to coat the pork tenderloin.
4. One tablespoon of olive oil should be drizzled over the pork tenderloin.
5. Cook the pork tenderloin on the grill for 20 to 25 minutes, or until an instant-read thermometer registers 145 degrees Fahrenheit.
6. After 5-10 minutes resting time, take the pork tenderloin off the grill and slice it into 1/2-inch-thick slices.
7. Turn the oven temperature up to 400 degrees Fahrenheit.
8. Combine the carrots and parsnips with 2 tablespoons of olive oil in a large bowl.
9. Put in as much salt and pepper as you want.
10. Put the veggies on a baking sheet in a single layer.
11. Cook the veggies in the oven for 20 to 25 minutes, or until they reach the desired tenderness and colour.
12. Toss the roasted carrots and parsnips with the sliced pork tenderloin and serve.

Calories: 335
Carbohydrates: 20g
Protein: 29g
Fat: 16g

LEMON HERB ROASTED CHICKEN WITH GREEN BEANS

SERVINGS: 4
PREPARATION TIME: 10 minutes

INGREDIENTS

- 4 chicken breasts, bone-in and skin-on
- 1 lb fresh green beans, trimmed
- 3 tbsp olive oil
- 2 lemons, sliced
- 4 cloves garlic, minced
- 2 tbsp fresh rosemary, finely chopped
- 2 tbsp fresh thyme, finely chopped
- 1 tsp salt
- 1/2 tsp black pepper

INSTRUCTIONS

1. Turn the oven temperature up to 400 degrees Fahrenheit (200 degrees Celsius).
2. Olive oil, garlic, rosemary, thyme, salt, and pepper should all be mixed together in a big bowl. Toss everything together.
3. Place the chicken breasts in the bowl and toss them around so that they are well covered in the herb mixture.
4. Spread the chicken breasts, skin side up, on a baking sheet. Cover the chicken with the lemon slices.
5. Prepare an oven to 400 degrees and roast the chicken for 40 minutes.
6. After 40 minutes, combine the chicken breasts with the pan juices and add the green beans, which have been trimmed.
7. After the chicken is fully done and the green beans are soft but still crisp, place the baking sheet back in the oven and roast for another 10 to 12 minutes.
8. After the timer goes off, take the chicken and green beans out of the oven and let them rest for 5 minutes before serving.

Calories: 450
Carbs: 12g
Protein: 50g
Fat: 22g

LOW FODMAP BEEF AND BROCCOLI STIR-FRY WITH RICE NOODLES

SERVINGS: 4
PREPARATION TIME: 30 minutes

INGREDIENTS

- 8 oz. rice noodles
- 1 lb. flank steak, thinly sliced
- 3 tbsp. low FODMAP soy sauce
- 2 tbsp. rice vinegar
- 2 tbsp. maple syrup
- 2 tbsp. sesame oil
- 1 tbsp. cornstarch
- 1 tbsp. grated ginger
- 2 cloves garlic, minced
- 1 head broccoli, chopped
- 1 red bell pepper, sliced
- 2 tbsp. chopped scallions, for garnish

INSTRUCTIONS

1. Noodles should be prepared in accordance with the package's directions and then put aside.
2. Blend the sauce ingredients (soy sauce, rice vinegar, maple syrup, sesame oil, cornstarch, ginger, and garlic) in a small bowl.
3. A good amount of oil should be heated over high heat in a big pan or wok. Slice the steak and cook it for about two minutes on each side, or until it is browned.
4. After about 2 to 3 minutes, or until the broccoli and bell pepper are just beginning to soften, add the veggies to the pan.
5. After the sauce has thickened and the veggies are covered, pour it into the pan and give everything a good swirl.
6. Lastly, throw in the cooked rice noodles and serve.
7. Serve immediately while still hot, and top with sliced scallions.

Calories: 475
Carbs: 52g
Protein: 28g
Fat: 18g

PAN-SEARED SCALLOPS WITH ROASTED BRUSSELS SPROUTS AND SWEET POTATO MASH

SERVINGS: 2
PREPARATION TIME: 30 minutes

INGREDIENTS

- 6 large scallops, cleaned and patted dry
- 1/2 lb Brussels sprouts, trimmed and halved
- 1 medium-sized sweet potato, peeled and cubed
- 2 tablespoons olive oil, divided
- 1/2 teaspoon dried thyme
- Salt and pepper to taste

INSTRUCTIONS

1. Turn the oven temperature up to 400F (200C).
2. Stir the Brussels sprouts, thyme, salt, and pepper together in a mixing dish with 1 tablespoon of olive oil. Roast them for 20-25 minutes, until they are soft and beginning to color.
3. Boil the sweet potato until it is soft in a medium saucepan, then drain and mash it with a fork or a potato masher. Sprinkle salt and pepper to taste.
4. Get a skillet hot over medium heat while the Brussels sprouts roast. Drop in the last tablespoon of olive oil.
5. Season the scallops with salt and pepper and then pat them dry with a paper towel.
6. Cook the scallops for two to three minutes on each side in a

heated pan until they are golden brown and opaque in the center.

7. Scallops should be served on a bed of sweet potato mash and roasted Brussels sprouts.

Calories: 341
Carbohydrates: 26g
Protein: 23g
Fat: 17g

HERB MARINATED LAMB CHOPS WITH GRILLED EGGPLANT AND RED PEPPER

SERVINGS: 4
PREPARATION TIME: 30 minutes (plus 2-3 hours for marinating)

INGREDIENTS

- 8 lamb chops
- 1 large eggplant, sliced
- 1 red bell pepper, sliced
- 2 tablespoons olive oil
- 2 tablespoons red wine vinegar
- 2 tablespoons fresh lemon juice
- 2 garlic cloves, minced
- 1 tablespoon dried oregano
- 1 tablespoon dried thyme
- Salt and pepper, to taste

INSTRUCTIONS

1. Olive oil, red wine vinegar, lemon juice, garlic, oregano, thyme, salt, and pepper should be mixed together in a small dish to form the marinade.
2. Marinate the lamb chops by placing them in a shallow dish and pouring the marinade over them, then flipping to coat.

Wrap the dish in plastic and chill it in the fridge for at least two hours, preferably longer.

3. Prepare a grill with medium-high heat. Pull the lamb chops out of the marinade and throw away the liquid.
4. Cook the lamb chops on the grill for three to four minutes each side, or until they achieve the doneness you choose.
5. Rub the eggplant and red pepper slices with olive oil and season with salt and pepper while the lamb chops are roasting. Cook the veggies on the grill for about three minutes each side, or until they reach the desired tenderness and charred flavor.
6. Roasted eggplant and red peppers are perfect accompaniments to grilled lamb chops.

Calories per serving: 350
Carbohydrates : 12g
Protein: 25g
Fat: 22-25g

TOMATO BASIL CHICKEN

SERVINGS: 4
PREPARATION TIME: 35 minutes

INGREDIENTS
- 4 boneless, skinless chicken breasts
- 2 cups canned diced tomatoes (without onion or garlic)
- 1/4 cup fresh basil, chopped
- 2 tablespoons olive oil
- Salt and pepper to taste

INSTRUCTIONS
1. In a skillet, heat olive oil over medium heat.
2. Season chicken breasts with salt and pepper and cook for 5-6 minutes per side until browned.
3. Add diced tomatoes and fresh basil to the skillet. Cook for an additional 5 minutes.
4. Serve chicken topped with tomato basil sauce.

Calories: 220
Carbs: 5g
Protein: 28g
Fat: 10g

LOW FODMAP SPAGHETTI SQUASH WITH TURKEY MEATBALLS AND TOMATO SAUCE

SERVINGS: 4
PREPARATION TIME: 45 minutes

INGREDIENTS
- 1 medium spaghetti squash
- 1 pound ground turkey
- 1/2 cup gluten-free breadcrumbs
- 1 egg
- 2 tablespoons chopped fresh parsley
- 1 teaspoon dried oregano
- 1/2 teaspoon garlic powder
- 1/4 teaspoon salt
- 1/4 teaspoon black pepper
- 1 tablespoon olive oil
- 1/2 cup low FODMAP tomato sauce
- Fresh basil, for garnish

INSTRUCTIONS
1. Get ready an oven preheated to 375 degrees Fahrenheit (190 degrees Celsius).
2. The spaghetti squash has to be halved longitudinally and the seeds scraped out.
3. The spaghetti squash should be baked for 30 to 40 minutes with the sliced side down until soft.
4. Mix the turkey, breadcrumbs, egg, herbs (parsley, oregano, garlic powder, salt, and pepper), and seasonings (in a big bowl). The ingredients must be well blended, therefore mixing is required.

5. Make meatballs with a diameter of approximately 1 1/2 inches from the mixture.
6. The olive oil should be heated in a large pan over medium heat. It should take around 5 minutes to brown the meatballs on both sides after adding them to the pan.
7. Cooking the meatballs in the tomato sauce is a great way to ensure that they are well covered with sauce. Simmer, covered, for 10–15 minutes, or until meatballs are done.
8. Put the strands of spaghetti squash into a serving dish by scraping them with a fork.
9. Turkey meatballs and tomato sauce go well on spaghetti squash.
10. Sprinkle with chopped fresh basil.

Carbs: 19g
Protein: 29g
Fat: 10g

GRILLED LEMON HERB CHICKEN

SERVINGS: 4
PREPARATION TIME: 30 minutes

INGREDIENTS
- 4 boneless, skinless chicken breasts
- 2 tablespoons olive oil
- 1 lemon (juice and zest)
- 2 teaspoons dried oregano
- Salt and pepper to taste

INSTRUCTIONS
1. In a bowl, combine olive oil, lemon juice, lemon zest, dried oregano, salt, and pepper.
2. Marinate chicken breasts in the mixture for 15 minutes.
3. Preheat grill to medium-high heat.
4. Grill chicken for 6-8 minutes per side or until cooked through.
5. Serve with your choice of low-FODMAP sides.

Calories: 220
Carbs: 2g
Protein: 30g
Fat: 10g

TURKEY AND CRANBERRY LETTUCE WRAPS

SERVINGS: 4
PREPARATION TIME: 20 minutes

INGREDIENTS
- 1 pound ground turkey
- 1/2 cup cranberry sauce (made with glucose syrup)
- 1/4 cup green onions (green parts only), chopped
- 8 large lettuce leaves (e.g., iceberg or butter lettuce)
- Salt and pepper to taste

INSTRUCTIONS
1. In a skillet, cook ground turkey over medium heat until browned.
2. Add cranberry sauce, green onions, salt, and pepper. Cook

for 2-3 minutes until heated through.

3. Spoon the turkey mixture into lettuce leaves and serve.

Calories: 230
Carbs: 17g
Protein: 21g
Fat: 9g

FISH

CILANTRO LIME GRILLED FISH WITH ROASTED CAULIFLOWER AND QUINOA

SERVINGS: 4
PREPARATION TIME: 30 minutes

INGREDIENTS
- 4 tilapia fillets
- 1/4 cup fresh lime juice
- 2 tablespoons olive oil
- 2 cloves garlic, minced
- 1/4 cup chopped fresh cilantro
- Salt and pepper, to taste
- 1 head cauliflower, cut into florets
- 2 tablespoons olive oil
- 1 cup quinoa, rinsed

INSTRUCTIONS
1. Prepare a grill with medium-high heat.
2. Lime juice, olive oil, garlic, cilantro, salt, and pepper are combined in a small bowl and whisked together.
3. Put the tilapia fillets in a shallow dish and pour the lime juice mixture over the top. Let marinate for 10-15 minutes while you prepare the cauliflower.
4. Mix the cauliflower florets with olive oil, salt, and pepper. In a 400°F oven, roast them in a single layer for 20 to 25 minutes, tossing them about halfway through cooking, until golden brown and soft.
5. Meanwhile, in a medium saucepan, bring the water to a boil. The cauliflower may go from the oven to the water. Stir in the quinoa. Turn the heat down to low and cover the pot. For best results, cover and simmer for 15–20 minutes, or until all the water is absorbed and the quinoa is soft.
6. Cook the tilapia fillets on the grill for three to four minutes each side, or until opaque throughout.
7. Serve the grilled fish over a bed of quinoa with roasted cauliflower on the side.

Calories: 280
Carbs: 36g
Protein: 29g
Fat: 12g

BAKED SWEET POTATO WITH LOW FODMAP TUNA SALAD

2 SERVINGS:
PREPARATION TIME: 10 minutes

INGREDIENTS
- 2 medium sweet potatoes
- 1 can of tuna in water, drained
- 1/4 cup of mayonnaise (low FODMAP, if needed)
- 1 tablespoon of Dijon mustard
- 2 tablespoons of chopped chives
- Salt and pepper to taste

INSTRUCTIONS
1. Preheat the oven to 400°F (200°C).

2. Scrub the sweet potatoes and pierce them a few times with a fork.

3. Place the sweet potatoes on a baking sheet lined with parchment paper and bake for 45 minutes, or until they are tender.

4. While the sweet potatoes are baking, prepare the tuna salad. In a small mixing bowl, mix together the drained tuna, mayonnaise, Dijon mustard, chopped chives, salt, and pepper.

5. Once the sweet potatoes are done, remove them from the oven and let them cool for a few minutes.

6. Cut open the sweet potatoes and top them with the tuna salad mixture.

Calories: 344
Carbs: 35g
Protein: 13g
Fat: 16g

LOW FODMAP TUNA AND AVOCADO SALAD

SERVINGS: 2
PREPARATION TIME: 10 minutes

INGREDIENTS
- 1 can of tuna, drained
- 1 small avocado, diced
- 1/4 cup of chopped celery
- 1/4 cup of chopped red bell pepper
- 2 tbsp of chopped fresh parsley

- 2 tbsp of mayonnaise
- 1 tbsp of lemon juice
- Salt and pepper to taste

INSTRUCTIONS
1. In a medium bowl, combine the tuna, avocado, celery, red bell pepper, and parsley.

2. In a small bowl, whisk together the mayonnaise and lemon juice until smooth.

3. Pour the mayonnaise mixture over the tuna and avocado mixture and stir until evenly coated.

4. Season with salt and pepper to taste.

5. Serve the tuna and avocado salad on a bed of lettuce leaves, if desired.

Calories: 253
Carbs: 8g
Protein: 17g
Fat: 18g

SHRIMP AND AVOCADO SALAD

SERVINGS: 2
PREPARATION TIME: 15 minutes

INGREDIENTS
- 1/2 pound large shrimp, peeled and deveined
- 1 avocado, diced
- 2 cups mixed salad greens
- 2 tablespoons olive oil
- 1 lemon (juice and zest)

- Salt and pepper to taste

INSTRUCTIONS

1. In a skillet, cook shrimp over medium heat for 2-3 minutes per side until pink.
2. In a large bowl, combine diced avocado, mixed salad greens, olive oil, lemon juice, lemon zest, salt, and pepper.
3. Add cooked shrimp to the salad mixture.
4. Toss and serve.

Calories: 310
Carbs: 9g
Protein: 20g
Fat: 24g

GRILLED SALMON WITH ROASTED VEGETABLES

SERVINGS: 4
PREPARATION TIME: 30 minutes

INGREDIENTS

- 4 salmon fillets (4-6 oz each)
- 2 cups broccoli florets
- 2 cups sliced zucchini
- 2 cups sliced bell peppers
- 1/4 cup olive oil
- 2 tbsp lemon juice
- 1 tsp dried basil
- 1 tsp dried oregano
- Salt and pepper to taste

INSTRUCTIONS

1. Turn the temperature on the oven to 400 degrees Fahrenheit (200 degrees Celsius).

2. Olive oil, lemon juice, dried basil, dried oregano, salt, and pepper are mixed together in a bowl with olive oil.
3. Place the broccoli florets, sliced zucchini, and sliced bell peppers in a separate dish. Use half of the olive oil mixture to toss the vegetables.
4. Place the veggies in an even layer on a baking sheet, then roast in the oven for about 20 minutes, or until the vegetables are soft.
5. In the meanwhile, bring the grill to a medium-high temperature.
6. Use a pastry brush to apply the remaining olive oil mixture on the salmon fillets.
7. Grill the salmon for 4-5 minutes each side, or until cooked through.
8. Serve the grilled fish with the roasted veggies.

Calories: 392
Carbs: 10g
Protein: 35g
Fat: 24g

GRILLED SHRIMP WITH QUINOA SALAD

SERVINGS: 4
PREPARATION TIME: 20 minutes

INGREDIENTS
For the Shrimp
- 1 pound large shrimp, peeled and deveined
- 1 tablespoon olive oil
- 2 garlic cloves, minced
- 1 teaspoon paprika
- Salt and pepper, to taste
- 4 skewers
For the Quinoa Salad
- 1 cup quinoa
- 2 cups water
- 1/2 teaspoon salt
- 1 red bell pepper, chopped
- 1 yellow bell pepper, chopped
- 1/2 cup chopped red onion
- 1/2 cup chopped fresh parsley
- 1/4 cup chopped fresh mint
- 1/4 cup olive oil
- 2 tablespoons lemon juice
- Salt and pepper, to taste

INSTRUCTIONS
1. Prepare the grill for cooking over medium-high heat.
2. Toss the shrimp with some olive oil, garlic, paprika, salt, and pepper before placing them in a medium bowl. Skewer the shrimp using thread or skewers.
3. Put the shrimp skewers on the grill and cook for about three to four minutes on each side, or until the shrimp become pink and are fully cooked.
4. While the shrimp are boiling, drain the quinoa in a colander with a fine mesh and run it under cold water. Place the quinoa, water, and salt in a pot of medium size, and then bring the mixture to a boil over high heat. After 15–20 minutes, or until the water is absorbed and the quinoa is cooked, reduce the heat to low, cover, and simmer the mixture.
5. Mix together the cooked quinoa, the red bell pepper, the yellow bell pepper, the red onion, the parsley, and the mint in a large bowl.
6. Olive oil, lemon juice, salt, and pepper should be mixed together in a small basin using a whisk. When the dressing has been drizzled over the quinoa salad, give it a good spin to cover everything.
7. As a side dish to the quinoa salad, serve the grilled shrimp.

Calories: per serving 377
Carbohydrates: 28g
Protein: 27g
Fat: 17g

BAKED COD WITH LEMON AND HERBS

SERVINGS: 2
PREPARATION TIME: 20 minutes

INGREDIENTS
- 2 cod fillets
- 2 tablespoons olive oil
- 1 lemon (juice and zest)
- 2 tablespoons fresh parsley, chopped
- Salt and pepper to taste

INSTRUCTIONS
1. Preheat oven to 375°F (190°C).
2. Place cod fillets on a baking sheet lined with parchment paper.
3. Drizzle olive oil over cod, then sprinkle with lemon juice, lemon zest, fresh parsley, salt, and pepper.
4. Bake for 15-20 minutes until fish flakes easily with a fork.
5. Serve with your favorite low-FODMAP side dishes.

Calories: 220
Carbs: 1g
Protein: 25g
Fat: 13g

TERIYAKI GLAZED SALMON

SERVINGS: 2
PREPARATION TIME: 25 minutes

INGREDIENTS
- 2 salmon fillets
- 1/4 cup gluten-free teriyaki sauce (check for FODMAP-friendly version)
- 2 tablespoons sesame seeds
- Salt and pepper to taste

INSTRUCTIONS
1. Preheat oven to 375°F (190°C).
2. Place salmon fillets on a baking sheet lined with parchment paper.
3. Brush salmon with gluten-free teriyaki sauce and sprinkle with sesame seeds, salt, and pepper.
4. Bake for 12-15 minutes until salmon flakes easily with a fork.
5. Serve hot.

Calories: 280
Carbs: 10g
Protein: 30g
Fat: 13g

LEMON HERB SALMON SALAD

SERVINGS: 2
PREPARATION TIME: 25 minutes

INGREDIENTS
- 2 salmon fillets
- 4 cups mixed salad greens
- 1 lemon (juice and zest)
- 2 tablespoons olive oil
- 1 tablespoon fresh dill, chopped
- Salt and pepper to taste

INSTRUCTIONS
1. Preheat oven to 375°F (190°C).
2. Place salmon fillets on a baking sheet lined with parchment paper.
3. In a small bowl, whisk together lemon juice, lemon zest, olive oil, fresh dill, salt, and pepper.
4. Brush the salmon fillets with the lemon herb mixture.
5. Bake for 12-15 minutes until salmon is cooked through.
6. Serve over mixed salad greens.

Calories: 330
Carbs: 7g
Protein: 26g
Fat: 23g

TUNA SALAD LETTUCE WRAPS

SERVINGS: 2
PREPARATION TIME: 15 minutes

INGREDIENTS
- 1 can of low FODMAP tuna, drained
- 1/4 cup of mayonnaise
- 1 tablespoon of Dijon mustard
- 2 tablespoons of chopped scallions (green part only)
- Salt and pepper to taste
- 4 large lettuce leaves
- 1/2 cup of sliced cucumber
- 1/2 cup of shredded carrots

INSTRUCTIONS
1. Combine the tuna that has been drained, the mayonnaise, the Dijon mustard, and the chopped scallions in a small mixing dish. Combine thoroughly.
2. Salt and pepper may be added to taste as a seasoning.
3. Arrange the lettuce leaves on a dish, and then dollop the tuna salad on top of each individual leaf.
4. Sliced cucumber and shredded carrots should be placed on top of each lettuce wrap.
5. Wrap the ingredients in the lettuce leaves, and serve them up right away.

Calories: 219 per serving
Carbohydrates: 5g
Protein: 18g
Fat: 14g

GRILLED SALMON WITH ROASTED SWEET POTATO

SERVINGS: 2
PREPARATION TIME: 40 minutes

INGREDIENTS

- 2 salmon fillets
- 2 medium sweet potatoes, peeled and cubed
- 2 tbsp olive oil
- 1 tbsp maple syrup
- 1 tbsp low FODMAP soy sauce
- 1 tsp grated ginger
- 1 tsp minced garlic
- Salt and pepper to taste
- Fresh parsley for garnish

INSTRUCTIONS

1. Turn the temperature on the oven to 400 degrees Fahrenheit (200 degrees Celsius).
2. Mix the sweet potatoes with a dash of salt and pepper, along with a tablespoon of olive oil. Roast them in the oven for 25 to 30 minutes, or until they are soft and have a little browning on them. Spread them out in a single layer on a baking sheet.
3. In the meanwhile, combine the remaining tablespoon of olive oil, the remaining tablespoon of maple syrup, the remaining tablespoon of soy sauce, ginger, and garlic. The salmon fillets should be seasoned with salt and pepper, and then the seasoning combination should be brushed over both sides of the fillets.
4. Prepare a grill pan by heating it over a medium-high flame. Add the salmon fillets and cook for three to four minutes on each side, or until they have reached the amount of doneness that you choose.
5. Salmon that has been grilled should be served with sweet potatoes that have been baked and topped with fresh parsley.

Calories: 375
Carbs: 25g
Protein: 28g, Fat: 18g

BAKED SALMON WITH DILL SAUCE

SERVINGS: 4
PREPARATION TIME: 25 minutes

INGREDIENTS

- 4 salmon fillets
- 1/4 cup lactose-free yogurt
- 1 tablespoon fresh dill, chopped
- 1 lemon (juice and zest)
- Salt and pepper to taste

INSTRUCTIONS

1. Preheat oven to 375°F (190°C).
2. Place salmon fillets on a baking sheet lined with parchment paper.
3. In a bowl, mix yogurt, fresh dill, lemon juice, lemon zest, salt, and pepper.
4. Spread the yogurt mixture over the salmon.
5. Bake for 15-20 minutes or until salmon flakes easily with a fork.

Calories: 250
Carbs: 2g
Protein: 26g
Fat: 15g

GRILLED SHRIMP AND VEGETABLE SKEWERS

SERVINGS: 4
PREPARATION TIME: 30 minutes

INGREDIENTS
- 1 pound large shrimp, peeled and deveined
- 2 bell peppers (red and yellow), cut into chunks
- Zucchini, sliced into rounds
- 2 tablespoons olive oil
- 2 tablespoons fresh basil, chopped
- Salt and pepper to taste

INSTRUCTIONS
1. Preheat grill to medium-high heat.
2. Thread shrimp, bell peppers, and zucchini alternately onto skewers.
3. Brush with olive oil, sprinkle with fresh basil, salt, and pepper.
4. Grill for 2-3 minutes per side until shrimp is pink and vegetables are tender.

Calories: 210
Carbs: 6g
Protein: 25g
Fat: 10g

LEMON GARLIC SHRIMP SCAMPI

SERVINGS: 2
PREPARATION TIME: 20 minutes

INGREDIENTS
- 8 ounces gluten-free spaghetti (or rice noodles)
- 1/2 pound large shrimp, peeled and deveined
- 2 tablespoons olive oil
- 3 cloves garlic, minced
- 1 lemon (juice and zest)
- 2 tablespoons fresh parsley, chopped

INSTRUCTIONS
1. Cook gluten-free spaghetti according to package instructions.
2. In a skillet, heat olive oil over medium heat. Add minced garlic and cook for 1 minute.
3. Add shrimp and cook for 2-3 minutes per side until pink.
4. Toss cooked spaghetti with lemon juice, lemon zest, fresh parsley, salt, and pepper.
5. Serve shrimp over the spaghetti.

Calories: 380
Carbs: 40g
Protein: 25g
Fat: 15g

SALMON AND DILL ZUCCHINI NOODLES

SERVINGS: 2
PREPARATION TIME: 25 minutes

INGREDIENTS

- 2 salmon fillets
- 2 large zucchinis, spiralized into noodles
- 2 tablespoons olive oil
- 2 tablespoons fresh dill, chopped
- 1 lemon (juice and zest)
- Salt and pepper to taste

INSTRUCTIONS

1. Preheat oven to 375°F (190°C).
2. Place salmon fillets on a baking sheet lined with parchment paper.
3. Drizzle olive oil over salmon, then sprinkle with fresh dill, lemon juice, lemon zest, salt, and pepper.
4. Bake for 12-15 minutes until salmon is cooked to your liking.
5. Serve over zucchini noodles.

Calories: 350
Carbs: 10g
Protein: 30g
Fat: 22g

LOW FODMAP SUSHI ROLLS WITH CRAB AND CUCUMBER

SERVINGS: 4
PREPARATION TIME: 30 minutes

INGREDIENTS

- 4 sheets of nori seaweed
- 2 cups of sushi rice
- 2 tablespoons of rice vinegar
- 2 tablespoons of sugar
- 1 teaspoon of salt
- 8 oz of cooked crab meat
- 1 small cucumber, peeled and sliced into thin strips
- 1 tablespoon of mayonnaise (low FODMAP)
- 1 tablespoon of gluten-free soy sauce
- 1 teaspoon of wasabi (optional)
- Pickled ginger (optional)

INSTRUCTIONS

1. Cook the sushi rice in accordance with the instructions provided on the box, and then let it to cool to room temperature.
2. Rice vinegar, sugar, and salt should all be combined in a small bowl and stirred together until the sugar and salt have dissolved.
3. Once the sushi rice has cooled, add the vinegar mixture and toss it together until it is completely incorporated.
4. Place a sheet of nori seaweed with the glossy side facing down on a sushi rolling mat.
5. On top of the nori seaweed, spread a thin layer of rice, being

sure to leave a border of about 1 inch at the top edge.

6. On top of the rice, arrange a strip of crab meat and several slices of cucumber.
7. Tightly roll the sushi using the mat as a guide so that it has the proper form.
8. Proceed with the remaining Components in the same manner.
9. Use a sharp knife to slice the sushi rolls into pieces that are suitable for eating immediately.
10. Mayonnaise, wasabi, gluten-free soy sauce, and pickled ginger should be served with the dish (if desired).

Calories: 328
Carbs: 60g
Protein: 12g
Fat: 3g

VEGETABLES

QUINOA-STUFFED BELL PEPPERS

SERVINGS: 4
PREPARATION TIME: 45 minutes

INGREDIENTS
- 4 bell peppers, tops removed and seeds removed
- 1 cup cooked quinoa
- 1 cup ground turkey (cooked)
- 1 cup canned diced tomatoes (without onion or garlic)
- 1/2 cup lactose-free cheddar cheese, shredded
- 1/4 cup fresh parsley, chopped
- Salt and pepper to taste

INSTRUCTIONS
1. Preheat oven to 375°F (190°C).
2. In a bowl, combine cooked quinoa, ground turkey, diced tomatoes, lactose-free cheddar cheese, parsley, salt, and pepper.
3. Stuff each bell pepper with the quinoa mixture.
4. Place stuffed peppers in a baking dish and cover with foil.
5. Bake for 25-30 minutes until peppers are tender.
6. Remove foil and bake for an additional 10 minutes to melt the cheese.

Calories: 330
Carbs: 27g
Protein: 26g
Fat: 14g

SPINACH AND FETA OMELETTE

SERVINGS: 2
PREPARATION TIME: 15 minutes

INGREDIENTS
- 4 large eggs
- 1 cup fresh spinach, chopped
- 1/4 cup lactose-free feta cheese, crumbled
- 2 tablespoons olive oil
- Salt and pepper to taste

INSTRUCTIONS
1. In a bowl, beat the eggs and season with salt and pepper.
2. Heat olive oil in a non-stick skillet over medium heat.
3. Add chopped spinach and cook for 2 minutes until wilted.
4. Pour the beaten eggs into the skillet and cook until the edges set.
5. Sprinkle feta cheese evenly over one half of the omelette.
6. Fold the other half over the cheese and cook until the cheese melts.

Calories: 280
Carbs: 1g
Protein: 17g
Fat: 23g

QUINOA AND ROASTED VEGETABLE SALAD

SERVINGS: 4
PREPARATION TIME: 40 minutes

INGREDIENTS
- 1 cup quinoa
- 2 cups water
- 2 cups mixed low-FODMAP roasted vegetables (e.g., carrots, zucchini, bell peppers)
- 2 tablespoons olive oil
- 2 tablespoons fresh lemon juice
- 1 tablespoon fresh parsley, chopped
- Salt and pepper to taste

INSTRUCTIONS
1. Cook quinoa according to package instructions.
2. Toss roasted vegetables with olive oil, lemon juice, parsley, salt, and pepper.
3. Serve quinoa topped with roasted vegetables.

Calories: 280
Carbs: 40g
Protein: 6g
Fat: 11g

GARLIC ROASTED SHRIMP WITH ASPARAGUS AND BROWN RICE

SERVINGS: 4
PREPARATION TIME: 30 minutes

INGREDIENTS
- 1 lb large shrimp, peeled and deveined
- 1 lb asparagus, trimmed and cut into 2-inch pieces
- 4 garlic cloves, minced
- 2 tbsp olive oil
- Salt and pepper
- 2 cups cooked brown rice

INSTRUCTIONS
1. Turn the oven temperature up to 400 degrees Fahrenheit.
2. Toss the shrimp and asparagus with the olive oil and chopped garlic in a large basin until everything is well covered.
3. Add pepper and salt to taste.
4. On a baking sheet, arrange the shrimp and asparagus in a single layer.
5. Prepare for 10-12 minutes in the oven, or until the shrimp are pink and fully cooked and the asparagus is soft.
6. Place the shrimp and asparagus on top of cooked brown rice and serve.

Calories: 280
Carbohydrates: 28g
Protein: 28g
Fat: 7g

VEGETABLE RICE

SERVINGS: 4
PREPARATION TIME: 25 minutes

INGREDIENTS
- 2 cups cooked brown rice
- 1 tablespoon garlic-infused oil
- 2 small zucchinis, sliced
- 2 small carrots, sliced
- 1/2 red bell pepper, sliced
- 1/2 cup green beans, trimmed and halved
- 1 tablespoon grated fresh ginger
- 2 tablespoons low-sodium soy sauce
- 1 tablespoon rice vinegar
- Salt and pepper, to taste

INSTRUCTIONS
1. Warm the oil that has been flavored with garlic in a wok or a big frying pan over medium-high heat.
2. After adding the zucchini, carrots, red bell pepper, and green beans to the pan, stir-fry them for three to five minutes, or until the veggies have reached the desired texture.
3. Stir-frying will continue for one more minute once grated ginger is added to the pan.
4. Combine the low-sodium soy sauce and rice vinegar in a small bowl and mix together until smooth.
5. Once the rice is finished cooking, add it to the pan with the veggies and toss to mix everything.
6. After pouring the soy sauce mixture over the rice and veggies, toss everything together to ensure that it is distributed evenly.
7. Salt and pepper may be added to taste as a seasoning.
8. To be served hot.

Calories: 215
Carbohydrates: 41g
Protein: 6g, Fat: 3g

BAKED SWEET POTATO WITH LOW FODMAP TOPPINGS

SERVINGS: 2
PREPARATION TIME: 10 minutes

INGREDIENTS
- 2 medium sweet potatoes
- 1 tbsp olive oil
- Salt and pepper to taste
- 1/2 cup lactose-free sour cream
- 2 green onions, green parts only, thinly sliced
- 1/4 cup chopped fresh parsley
- 1/4 cup chopped fresh chives

INSTRUCTIONS
1. Turn the temperature on the oven to 400 degrees Fahrenheit (200 degrees Celsius).
2. Once they have been washed and pricked with a fork a few times, the sweet potatoes are ready to be baked.
3. Olive oil should be rubbed into the sweet potatoes, and then they should be seasoned with salt and pepper.

4. Bake for 45-50 minutes, or until tender.
5. Combine the sour cream that does not contain lactose, the green onions, the parsley, and the chives in a small bowl.
6. Once the sweet potatoes have been cooked through, slit them open and place a spoonful of the sour cream mixture into each one.
7. To be served hot.

Calories: 304
Carbs: 49g
Protein: 4g Fat: 11g

LOW FODMAP ZUCCHINI AND TOMATO QUICHE

SERVINGS: 6
PREPARATION TIME: 15 minutes

INGREDIENTS

- 1 pre-made gluten-free pie crust
- 2 tbsp. olive oil
- 2 small zucchinis, sliced
- 2 small tomatoes, sliced
- 4 large eggs
- 1 cup lactose-free milk
- 1/4 cup chopped fresh basil
- Salt and pepper to taste
- 1 cup shredded lactose-free cheese

INSTRUCTIONS

1. Get ready an oven preheated to 375 degrees Fahrenheit (190 degrees Celsius).
2. Olive oil should be heated in a pan over medium heat.
3. Sliced zucchinis should be added and cooked for 5 minutes, or until they are just soft.
4. Combine the eggs, lactose-free milk, basil, salt, and pepper in a bowl and whisk together.
5. Make use of a 9-inch pie plate to house the prepared pie dough.
6. Layer the pie crust with the cut tomatoes and zucchini.
7. Sprinkle the veggies with the egg mixture.
8. Shredded lactose-free cheese makes a delicious topping for the quiche.
9. For about 35-40 minutes in a preheated oven, or until the filling has set and the top is golden, bake the quiche.
10. You should wait a few minutes for the quiche to cool before cutting it.

Calories: 340
Carbohydrates: 22g
Protein: 13g
Fat: 23g

ROASTED BUTTERNUT SQUASH SOUP

SERVINGS: 4
PREPARATION TIME: 45 minutes

INGREDIENTS

- 1 butternut squash, peeled and cubed
- 2 carrots, peeled and chopped
- 2 cups low-sodium chicken or vegetable broth
- 1 cup canned coconut milk
- 1 tablespoon olive oil
- 1 teaspoon fresh ginger, grated
- Salt and pepper to taste

INSTRUCTIONS

1. Preheat oven to 400°F (200°C).
2. Toss butternut squash and carrots with olive oil, salt, and pepper. Roast for 30-35 minutes until tender.
3. In a blender, combine roasted vegetables, chicken or vegetable broth, coconut milk, and grated ginger. Blend until smooth.
4. Transfer to a pot and heat over medium heat until warmed through.

Calories: 210
Carbs: 24g
Protein: 3g
Fat: 13g

TOMATO AND BASIL ZUCCHINI NOODLES

SERVINGS: 2
PREPARATION TIME: 20 minutes

INGREDIENTS

- 2 large zucchinis, spiralized into noodles
- 1 cup canned diced tomatoes (without onion or garlic)
- 2 tablespoons olive oil
- 2 tablespoons fresh basil, chopped
- Salt and pepper to taste

INSTRUCTIONS

1. In a skillet, heat olive oil over medium heat.
2. Add zucchini noodles and cook for 2-3 minutes until slightly softened.
3. Add diced tomatoes, fresh basil, salt, and pepper. Cook for an additional 2-3 minutes.
4. Serve as a side dish or with your choice of protein.

Calories: 160
Carbs: 12g
Protein: 2g
Fat: 12g

GRILLED ZUCCHINI AND EGGPLANT STACK

SERVINGS: 4
PREPARATION TIME: 25 minutes

INGREDIENTS

- 2 zucchinis, sliced into rounds
- 2 small eggplants, sliced into rounds
- 2 tablespoons olive oil
- 1 teaspoon dried thyme
- Salt and pepper to taste

INSTRUCTIONS

1. Preheat grill to medium-high heat.
2. Toss zucchini and eggplant slices with olive oil, dried thyme, salt, and pepper.
3. Grill for 3-4 minutes per side until tender.
4. Stack zucchini and eggplant slices to create a tower.

Calories: 120
Carbs: 10g
Protein: 2g
Fat: 9g

GRILLED LEMON GARLIC ASPARAGUS

SERVINGS: 4
PREPARATION TIME: 15 minutes

INGREDIENTS

- 1 bunch of asparagus, trimmed
- 2 tablespoons olive oil
- 2 cloves garlic, minced
- 1 lemon (juice and zest)
- Salt and pepper to taste

INSTRUCTIONS

1. Preheat grill to medium-high heat.
2. Toss trimmed asparagus with olive oil, minced garlic, lemon juice, lemon zest, salt, and pepper.
3. Grill for 3-4 minutes per side until tender and slightly charred.

Calories: 70
Carbs: 4g
Protein: 2g
Fat: 6g

SCRAMBLED EGGS WITH SPINACH AND TOMATO

SERVINGS: 2
PREPARATION TIME: 15 minutes

INGREDIENTS

- 4 large eggs
- 1 cup fresh spinach, chopped
- 1 tomato, diced
- 1 tablespoon olive oil
- Salt and pepper to taste

INSTRUCTIONS

1. In a bowl, beat the eggs and season with salt and pepper.
2. Heat olive oil in a non-stick skillet over medium heat.
3. Add chopped spinach and diced tomato and cook for 2 minutes until wilted.
4. Pour beaten eggs into the skillet and cook, stirring, until eggs are set.

Calories: 210
Carbs: 5g
Protein: 13g
Fat: 15g

CUCUMBERS AND TOMATOES SALAD

SERVINGS: 4
PREPARATION TIME: 15 minutes

INGREDIENTS

- 2 cucumbers, sliced
- 2 tomatoes, diced
- 1/4 cup fresh parsley, chopped
- 2 tablespoons olive oil
- 1 tablespoon fresh lemon juice
- Salt and pepper to taste

INSTRUCTIONS

1. In a large bowl, combine sliced cucumbers, diced tomatoes, and chopped fresh parsley.
2. Drizzle with olive oil and fresh lemon juice.
3. Season with salt and pepper and toss to combine.
4. Serve as a refreshing side salad.

Calories: 80
Carbs: 6g
Protein: 2g
Fat: 6g

SPAGHETTI SQUASH WITH PESTO

SERVINGS: 4
PREPARATION TIME: 40 minutes

INGREDIENTS

- 1 spaghetti squash
- 1/2 cup homemade pesto (made without garlic)
- 2 tablespoons pine nuts, toasted
- Salt and pepper to taste

INSTRUCTIONS

1. Preheat oven to 375°F (190°C).
2. Cut the spaghetti squash in half lengthwise and remove the seeds.
3. Place squash halves, cut side down, on a baking sheet and roast for 30-35 minutes until tender.
4. Scrape the flesh of the squash into strands using a fork.
5. Toss the spaghetti squash with pesto, toasted pine nuts, salt, and pepper.

Calories: 280
Carbs: 15g
Protein: 4g
Fat: 24g

ROASTED RED PEPPER AND TOMATO SOUP

SERVINGS: 4
PREPARATION TIME: 45 minutes

INGREDIENTS

- 2 red bell peppers, roasted and peeled
- 4 large tomatoes
- 2 tablespoons olive oil
- 1 cup low-sodium chicken or vegetable broth
- 1 teaspoon fresh basil, chopped
- Salt and pepper to taste

INSTRUCTIONS

1. Preheat oven to 400°F (200°C).
2. Place red bell peppers and tomatoes on a baking sheet and drizzle with olive oil. Roast for 20-25 minutes until skin blisters.
3. Peel and chop roasted red peppers and tomatoes.
4. In a pot, combine chopped vegetables, chicken or vegetable broth, fresh basil, salt, and pepper. Simmer for 15-20 minutes.
5. Blend the soup until smooth.

Calories: 140
Carbs: 12g
Protein: 2g
Fat: 10g

BAKED TOFU WITH PEANUT SAUCE

SERVINGS: 4
PREPARATION TIME: 40 minutes

INGREDIENTS

- 1 block of firm tofu, cut into cubes
- 1/4 cup peanut butter (without added high-FODMAP **INGREDIENTS**)
- 2 tablespoons soy sauce (check for FODMAP-friendly version)
- 2 tablespoons rice vinegar
- 1 tablespoon sesame oil
- 1 teaspoon fresh ginger, minced
- Salt and pepper to taste

INSTRUCTIONS

1. Place tofu cubes on a baking sheet lined with parchment paper and bake for 25-30 minutes until crispy, 375°F (190°C).
2. In a bowl, whisk together all ingredient and toss baked tofu cubes in the peanut sauce.
3. Serve warm

Calories: 250
Carbs: 8g
Protein: 15g
Fat: 18g

DESSERT

BANANA AND BLUEBERRY SMOOTHIE BOWL

SERVINGS: 1
PREPARATION TIME: 10 minutes

INGREDIENTS
- 1 ripe banana
- 1/2 cup blueberries
- 1/2 cup lactose-free yogurt
- 1 tablespoon honey
- Gluten-free granola (check for low FODMAP)

INSTRUCTIONS
1. In a blender, combine the ripe banana, blueberries, lactose-free yogurt, and honey.
2. Blend until smooth.
3. Pour the smoothie into a bowl.
4. Sprinkle the top with gluten-free granola.
5. Serve and enjoy!

Calories: 350
Carbs: 80g
Protein: 7g
Fat: 3g

VANILLA ICE CREAM WITH FRESH STRAWBERRIES

SERVINGS: 4
PREPARATION TIME: 30 minutes (including cooling time)

INGREDIENTS
- 2 cups lactose-free vanilla ice cream
- 1 cup fresh strawberries, sliced
- 1 tablespoon sugar (optional)
- Fresh mint leaves for garnish

INSTRUCTIONS
1. In a bowl, mix the sliced strawberries with sugar (if desired) and let them sit for about 15 minutes.
2. Serve the vanilla ice cream in individual bowls.
3. Pour the marinated strawberries over the ice cream.
4. Garnish with fresh mint leaves and serve immediately.

Calories: 200
Carbs: 32g
Protein: 2g
Fat: 7g

CINNAMON-SPICED RICE PUDDING

SERVINGS: 4
PREPARATION TIME: 45 minutes

INGREDIENTS

- 1 cup Arborio rice
- 2 cups lactose-free milk
- 1/4 cup sugar
- 1 teaspoon ground cinnamon
- 1 teaspoon vanilla extract
- 1/4 cup sliced almonds (optional for garnish)

INSTRUCTIONS

1. In a saucepan, combine the Arborio rice, lactose-free milk, sugar, and ground cinnamon.
2. Cook over medium heat, stirring frequently, until the rice is tender and the mixture thickens (about 30-35 minutes).
3. Remove from heat and stir in the vanilla extract.
4. Let it cool before serving.
5. Garnish with sliced almonds if desired.

Calories: 300
Carbs: 56g
Protein: 8g
Fat: 5g

FODMAP-FRIENDLY CHOCOLATE MOUSSE

SERVINGS: 2
PREPARATION TIME: 20 minutes

INGREDIENTS

- 1/2 cup dark chocolate chips (check for low FODMAP)
- 1/2 cup lactose-free whipping cream
- 1/2 teaspoon vanilla extract
- 1 tablespoon powdered sugar (optional)
- Fresh raspberries for garnish

INSTRUCTIONS

1. Melt the dark chocolate chips in a microwave-safe bowl or using a double boiler.
2. In a separate bowl, whip the lactose-free whipping cream until stiff peaks form.
3. Gently fold the melted chocolate and vanilla extract into the whipped cream.
4. Add powdered sugar if desired for sweetness.
5. Spoon the chocolate mousse into serving glasses.
6. Refrigerate for at least 2 hours or until set.
7. Garnish with fresh raspberries before serving.

Calories: 380
Carbs: 25g
Protein: 3g
Fat: 30g

LEMON BLUEBERRY PARFAIT

SERVINGS: 2
PREPARATION TIME: 15 minutes

INGREDIENTS
- 1 cup lactose-free Greek yogurt
- 1 cup blueberries
- Zest of 1 lemon
- 1 tablespoon maple syrup (use pure maple syrup)
- Gluten-free granola (check for low FODMAP)

INSTRUCTIONS
1. In a bowl, mix the lactose-free Greek yogurt with lemon zest and maple syrup.
2. In serving glasses, layer the yogurt mixture, blueberries, and gluten-free granola.
3. Repeat the layers as desired.
4. Serve immediately or refrigerate until ready to enjoy.

Calories: 220
Carbs: 42g
Protein: 11g
Fat: 2g

RASPBERRY ALMOND CHIA PUDDING

SERVINGS: 2
PREPARATION TIME: 10 minutes (plus chilling time)

INGREDIENTS
- 1/4 cup chia seeds
- 1 cup lactose-free milk
- 1/2 cup fresh raspberries
- 2 tablespoons almond butter (without high-FODMAP **INGREDIENTS**)
- 1 tablespoon maple syrup (use pure maple syrup)

INSTRUCTIONS
1. In a bowl, combine chia seeds, lactose-free milk, almond butter, and maple syrup.
2. Stir well and refrigerate for at least 4 hours or overnight until the mixture thickens.
3. Serve topped with fresh raspberries.

Calories: 300
Carbs: 28g
Protein: 9g
Fat: 18g

PINEAPPLE COCONUT SORBET

SERVINGS: 4
PREPARATION TIME: 5 minutes (plus freezing time)

INGREDIENTS
- 2 cups frozen pineapple chunks
- 1/2 cup coconut milk (canned, without high-FODMAP additives)
- 2 tablespoons maple syrup (use pure maple syrup)

INSTRUCTIONS
1. In a blender, combine frozen pineapple chunks, coconut milk, and maple syrup.
2. Blend until smooth.
3. Transfer the mixture to a freezer-safe container and freeze for at least 2 hours or until it reaches a sorbet-like consistency.
4. Scoop and serve.

Calories: 150
Carbs: 28g
Protein: 1g
Fat: 5g

CHOCOLATE-DIPPED STRAWBERRIES

SERVINGS: 4
PREPARATION TIME: 20 minutes (plus cooling time)

INGREDIENTS
- 1 cup dark chocolate chips (check for low FODMAP)
- 1 cup strawberries
- 1 tablespoon coconut oil (optional)

INSTRUCTIONS
1. Line a baking sheet with parchment paper.
2. In a microwave-safe bowl or using a double boiler, melt the dark chocolate chips and coconut oil (if using) until smooth.
3. Dip each strawberry into the melted chocolate, allowing any excess to drip off.
4. Place the dipped strawberries on the prepared baking sheet.
5. Allow the chocolate to cool and harden.
6. Serve as a sweet treat.

Calories: 180
Carbs: 25g
Protein: 2g
Fat: 9g

COCONUT RICE PUDDING WITH PASSION FRUIT

SERVINGS: 4
PREPARATION TIME: 40 minutes

INGREDIENTS
- 1 cup Arborio rice
- 2 cups coconut milk
- 1/4 cup sugar
- 1/2 teaspoon vanilla extract
- Pulp of 2 ripe passion fruits

INSTRUCTIONS
1. In a saucepan, combine the Arborio rice, coconut milk, and sugar.
2. Cook over medium heat, stirring frequently, until the rice is tender and the mixture thickens (about 30-35 minutes).
3. Remove from heat and stir in the vanilla extract.
4. Let it cool.
5. Serve in dessert bowls and top with passion fruit pulp.

Calories: 320
Carbs: 48g
Protein: 2g
Fat: 14g

ALMOND AND RASPBERRY MINI TARTS

SERVINGS: 6
PREPARATION TIME: 30 minutes

INGREDIENTS
For the Crust
- 1 1/2 cups almond flour
- 2 tablespoons maple syrup (use pure maple syrup)
- 2 tablespoons coconut oil, melted (without high-FODMAP additives)
- A pinch of salt

For the Filling
- 1/2 cup fresh raspberries
- 1/4 cup almond butter (without high-FODMAP **INGREDIENTS**)
- 2 tablespoons maple syrup (use pure maple syrup)
- 1/2 teaspoon vanilla extract

INSTRUCTIONS
For the Crust
1. Preheat the oven to 350°F (180°C).
2. In a bowl, combine almond flour, maple syrup, melted coconut oil, and a pinch of salt.
3. Press the mixture into mini tart pans, forming the crust.
4. Bake for about 10-12 minutes or until the crusts are lightly golden.

For the Filling
5. In a blender, combine fresh raspberries, almond butter, maple syrup, and vanilla extract.
6. Blend until smooth.

7. Spoon the raspberry-almond mixture into the cooled tart crusts.
8. Refrigerate until set.

Calories: 290
Carbs: 17g
Protein: 7g
Fat: 22g

CONCLUSION

Throughout the pages of this book, we have explored the intricacies of inflammation and its impact on our overall health and wellbeing. From the role of the gut microbiome to the importance of maintaining a balanced diet, we have uncovered a wealth of knowledge and practical tools for managing inflammation through food. Specifically, we have focused on the FODMAP diet, a dietary approach that has been shown to have anti-inflammatory properties and is particularly beneficial for those suffering from IBS.

The FODMAP diet emphasizes the importance of limiting certain types of carbohydrates that can be difficult to digest and may exacerbate inflammation. By following the guidelines of the FODMAP diet, individuals can manage their IBS symptoms and reduce inflammation, leading to improved digestive health and overall wellness. And with the wide range of delicious and nutritious recipes included in this book, readers can discover how to make the FODMAP diet an enjoyable and sustainable part of their daily routine.

By taking a proactive approach to our health and wellbeing, we can achieve greater control over our lives and improve our quality of life. With the knowledge and tools provided in this book, readers can embark on a journey towards better health and happiness, one meal at a time. Whether you are struggling with IBS or simply seeking to adopt a healthier lifestyle, the principles of an anti-inflammatory diet and the FODMAP approach can help you achieve your goals and thrive in all areas of your life.

21-DAY FOOD PLAN

The menu that follows serves as an illustration of how to match meals. With a little creativity, you can make as many as you want!

WEEK 1			
	MONDAY	*TUESDAY*	*WEDNESDAY*
BREAKFAST	SCRAMBLED EGGS WITH TOMATOES AND AVOCADO	GLUTEN-FREE YOGURT PARFAIT WITH LOW FODMAP FRUITS AND GRANOLA	MIXED BERRY OVERNIGHT OATS
LUNCH	CHICKEN AND VEGETABLE STIR-FRY	LOW FODMAP TUNA AND AVOCADO SALAD	BAKED SWEET POTATO
DINNER	CUCUMBER AND TOMATO SALAD	TERIYAKI GLAZED SALMON	TUNA SALAD LETTUCE WRAPS
EXTRA	VANILLA ICE CREAM WITH FRESH STRAWBERRIES	NO	LEMON BLUEBERRY PARFAIT

	THURSDAY	*FRIDAY*	*SATURDAY*	*SUNDAY*
BREAKFAST	BLUEBERRY PANCAKES	MIXED BERRY OVERNIGHT OATS	GLUTEN-FREE YOGURT PARFAIT WITH LOW FODMAP FRUITS AND GRANOLA	PEANUT BUTTER BANANA SMOOTHIE BOWL
LUNCH	BAKED TOFU WITH PEANUT SAUCE	GRILLED LEMON GARLIC ASPARAGUS	LEMON HERB SALMON SALAD	GRILLED LEMON HERB CHICKEN
DINNER	LOW FODMAP TUNA AND AVOCADO SALAD	BAKED SWEET POTATO	CHICKEN AND VEGETABLE STIR-FRY	TUNA SALAD LETTUCE WRAPS
EXTRA	NO	BAKED COD WITH LEMON AND HERBS	NO	BANANA AND BLUEBERRY SMOOTHIE BOWL

WEEK 2			
	MONDAY	*TUESDAY*	*WEDNESDAY*
BREAKFAST	CHIA SEED PUDDING	LOW-FODMAP PANCAKES	GLUTEN-FREE YOGURT PARFAIT WITH LOW FODMAP FRUITS AND

			GRANOLA
LUNCH	LOW FODMAP CHICKEN CAESAR SALAD	VEGETABLE RICE	ROASTED BUTTERNUT SQUASH SOUP
DINNER	QUINOA AND ROASTED VEGETABLE SALAD	LOW FODMAP SUSHI ROLLS WITH CRAB AND CUCUMBER	CUCUMBER AND TOMATO SALAD
EXTRA	NO	PINEAPPLE COCONUT SORBET	NO

	THURSDAY	FRIDAY	SATURDAY	SUNDAY
BREAKFAST	QUINOA BREAKFAST BOWL	MIXED BERRY OVERNIGHT OATS	BLUEBERRY PANCAKES	OMELETTE WITH SPINACH AND FETA
LUNCH	ROASTED BUTTERNUT SQUASH SOUP	VEGETABLE RICE	GRILLED LEMON GARLIC ASPARAGUS	BAKED TOFU WITH PEANUT SAUCE
DINNER	TUNA SALAD LETTUCE WRAPS	QUINOA AND ROASTED VEGETABLE SALAD	LOW FODMAP CHICKEN CAESAR SALAD	CUCUMBER AND TOMATO SALAD
EXTRA	BANANA AND BLUEBERRY SMOOTHIE BOWL	NO	LEMON BLUEBERRY PARFAIT	NO

WEEK 3			
	MONDAY	TUESDAY	WEDNESDAY
BREAKFAST	OMELETTE WITH SPINACH AND FETA	GLUTEN-FREE OATMEAL	CHIA SEED PUDDING WITH LOW FODMAP FRUITS AND COCONUT MILK
LUNCH	CHICKEN AND	TERIYAKI GLAZED	ROASTED

		VEGETABLE STIR-FRY	SALMON	BUTTERNUT SQUASH SOUP
DINNER		LOW FODMAP TUNA AND AVOCADO SALAD	LOW FODMAP SUSHI ROLLS WITH CRAB AND CUCUMBER	CHICKEN AND VEGETABLE STIR-FRY
EXTRA		PINEAPPLE COCONUT SORBET	NO	LEMON BLUEBERRY PARFAIT

	THURSDAY	*FRIDAY*	*SATURDAY*	*SUNDAY*
BREAKFAST	PEANUT BUTTER BANANA SMOOTHIE BOWL	CHIA SEED PUDDING	GLUTEN-FREE YOGURT PARFAIT WITH LOW FODMAP FRUITS AND GRANOLA	QUINOA BREAKFAST BOWL
LUNCH	QUINOA AND ROASTED VEGETABLE SALAD	TURKEY AND LETTUCE WRAP	CUCUMBER AND TOMATO SALAD	GRILLED CHICKEN WITH ROASTED VEGETABLES
DINNER	LOW FODMAP CHICKEN AND VEGETABLE SKEWERS	LOW FODMAP SUSHI ROLLS WITH CRAB AND CUCUMBER	TUNA SALAD LETTUCE WRAPS	TERIYAKI GLAZED SALMON
EXTRA	NO	CINNAMON-SPICED RICE PUDDING	NO	VANILLA ICE CREAM WITH FRESH STRAWBERRIES

Hi, I'm Robert

12/11/1972
Zodiac Sign, Scorpio
Height, 181 cm

Who am I ?

Robert is a journalist passionate about nutrition, diet, and exercise. From a young age, he has shown a keen interest in health and wellness, recognizing the importance of a balanced diet and an active lifestyle.

After obtaining a degree in journalism, Robert decided to specialize in the field of nutrition and fitness. He began studying various dietary theories and exploring the most effective approaches to maintaining a healthy lifestyle. During his educational journey, he learned the fundamentals of food science and developed a deep understanding of how food affects the body and mind.

With a solid knowledge base, Robert started writing articles on diets, nutrition, and training for various magazines and websites. He worked with industry experts and interviewed renowned nutritionists, dieticians, and personal trainers to gain a broader perspective on best practices in this field.

Robert's mission is to educate the public about adopting a healthy approach to nutrition and exercise. He believes that good nutrition is essential for achieving a balanced life and that regular physical activity is crucial for long-term well-being.

In addition to writing informative articles, Robert conducts in-depth research on diets and emerging food trends. He constantly seeks to stay updated on the latest scientific discoveries in the field of nutrition and exercise, in order to provide accurate, evidence-based information to his readers.

Robert's passion for nutrition and fitness extends to his personal life as well. He follows a balanced diet and regularly engages in physical activities to maintain fitness and overall well-being. He firmly believes that adopting a healthy lifestyle is an investment in one's future, bringing benefits not only physically but also mentally and emotionally.

Through his work, Robert aims to inspire others to take care of their health through mindful food choices and adequate physical activity. His hope is that the information he shares can help people improve their lives and achieve long-term wellness.

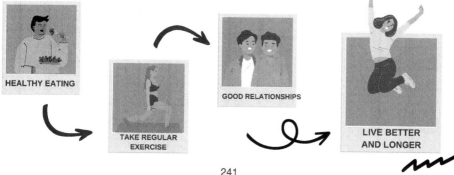

GRAB YOUR BONUSES!
SCAN THE QR CODE

A weight loss journal, a valuable tool for documenting and tracking weight loss progress, serves as an individual's personal log to record food intake, exercise routines, and lifestyle habits. By meticulously noting details like meals, calorie counts, portion sizes, exercise duration, and any other relevant factors, the journal provides a comprehensive overview of one's commitment to achieving a healthy weight.

Understanding nutritional content, ingredients, and sourcing empowers us to make healthy decisions that align with our needs. Transparency in the food industry and support for sustainable practices are also benefits. Make informed choices, promote better health, and support a healthier food environment.

Dish up delicious DASH-friendly meals that are perfect for any celebration, without compromising your health goals.

Getting regular exercise is critical to successful diet and feeling better. If you don't know how to get started, this guide can help you

SUPER BONUS: MEDITERRANEAN DIET COOKBOOK

FULL VERSION

In the pages of "Mediterranean Magic," embark on a tantalizing voyage through the sun-kissed lands of the Mediterranean, where vibrant flavors dance on your palate and nourish your body. This exquisite tome is more than just a cookbook; it's a celebration of the rich tapestry of cultures that have cultivated the renowned Mediterranean diet.

Within its beautifully illustrated pages, you'll discover an array of mouthwatering recipes crafted with fresh, wholesome ingredients sourced from land and sea. From the lush olive groves of Greece to the aromatic herb gardens of Italy, each recipe is a testament to the bountiful harvests and culinary traditions that have sustained generations.

**THANK YOU FOR CHOOSING THIS BOOK!
IF YOU ENJOYED IT, PLEASE CONSIDER LEAVING A REVIEW ON AMAZON, IT WILL TAKE LESS THAN A MINUTE.**

PLEASE, SCAN THE FOLLOWING QR CODE WITH YOUR MOBILE.

If you like the book, don't forget to let me know by scanning the following QR code and writing your review.

Thank you!

Notes

Printed in Great Britain
by Amazon